Carousel Animal Carving:
Patterns & Techniques

Bud Ellis & Rhonda Hoeckley

Sterling Publishing Co., Inc. New York

Library of Congress Cataloging-in-Publication Data

Ellis, Frank, 1936–
    Carousel animal carving : patterns & techniques / Frank Ellis &
Rhonda Hoeckley.
        p.   cm.
    Includes index.
    ISBN 0-8069--0305-8
    1. Wood-carving. 2. Merry-go-round art. 3. Animals in art.
    I. Hoeckley, Rhonda. II. Title.
TT199.7.E517 1998
731´.832—dc21   97–43002
                                                            CIP

10 9 8 7 6 5 4 3 2 1

Published by Sterling Publishing Company, Inc.
387 Park Avenue South, New York, N.Y. 10016
© 1998 by Frank Ellis
Distributed in Canada by Sterling Publishing
c/o Canadian Manda Group, One Atlantic Avenue, Suite 105
Toronto, Ontario, Canada M6K 3E7
Distributed in Great Britain and Europe by Cassell PLC
Wellington House, 125 Strand, London WC2R 0BB, England
Distributed in Australia by Capricorn Link (Australia) Pty Ltd.
P.O. Box 6651, Baulkham Hills, Business Centre, NSW 2153, Australia
Printed and Bound in China
All rights reserved

Sterling ISBN 0-8069-0305-8

The photograph on the title page was taken by Robin Hood

CONTENTS

ACKNOWLEDGMENTS

It takes help to make dreams come true. One of the people who helped to make my dream of teaching people to carve carousel animals come true is my wife, Johnnie, who spent many long hours helping to get our carousel business going.

From time to time, people enter our lives and share their skills and experience. One such person was James Bacon, who worked with us for several years. James is one of those people you meet once or twice in a lifetime who possesses a natural talent for carving. James always seems to know how to put that little something special into each animal.

Also, it would be impossible to express the extent of my gratitude to Rhonda Hoeckley. Little did I know what God had in store for me when I was asked if I could write a book on carving carousel animals. This is something I could not have accomplished if I did not have the good fortune to meet Rhonda. I told her about the book, and she said she could help. And help she did! Thank you God for sending this angel.

Without these people and all their talent and help, this book would not have been possible.

Bud Ellis

Writing a book is never a solo endeavor. Thanks go to my husband, Steve, who opened the door to carousel carving for me with a very special gift, and to Stephanie and Candace, for giving up a little bit of time with their Mommy so I could write. Thanks also go to my own mother, Orla, who gave me enough of her artist's eye to appreciate what a wonderful art form carousel carving really is.

A big thanks from both of us to Tom Cory, for taking such terrific photographs, and to Kathleen Bond, of K.B. Leather Art in Holland, Ohio, for contributing the wonderful patterns in Chapter 4.

Rhonda Hoeckley

PREFACE

A Teacher's Perspective

As jobs go, I must have one of the best. Every morning I get up, drive to work, and spend the day teaching people how to carve carousel animals. I often look back in wonder at how a carousel-carving school like Horsin' Around ever got started in Chattanooga, Tennessee—especially by me. It took a lot of steps in my life to get here, but there isn't anything I'd rather be doing than teaching people how to carve their own full-size carousel animals.

My first contact with carousels was during Sunday-afternoon picnics in Evansville, Indiana. Some of my best early memories are of eating fried chicken and potato salad in the park with my family on sunny Sunday afternoons, and then racing over to the old Philadelphia Toboggan Co. carousel in the Mesker Zoo for a ride.

My interest in art and woodcarving also started early, thanks to my mother. When I was a child, she spent endless hours carving small figures for friends in the neighborhood. Eventually, my interests led me to Indiana University for a degree in art education, and later to the University of Tennessee for a master's degree in metalsmithing.

One day while teaching art at the University of Tennessee, I came across an old carousel frame in an antique shop. By this time, I was spending a lot of my spare time carving large wooden figures, so I saw no reason why I couldn't carve carousel animals for this wonderful old carousel frame. As I sorted through the various parts of the old machine, I realized the band organ was missing and I inquired as to its whereabouts. That's when I was lucky enough to meet Charles Walker. Many people who are interested in carousels in this country know Charles Walker as one of the founders of the National Carousel Association, and one of the most knowledgeable people in the country about carousel history. He had purchased the organ and planned to restore it.

Realizing that the organ was in good hands, I started repairing and recarving Mr. Walker's many broken carousel horses. Through this work, I soon learned how the animals were built and carved by the master carvers at the turn of the century, and before long I started carving authentic carousel ani-

A selection of hand-carved carousel horses that are within the capabilities of most people.

mals on my own. By this time, I was tired from teaching art for so many years, and carving carousel animals helped me relax and escape from the pressures of my job.

Since carving big animals takes some space, I rented an old grocery store to work in and carved there at night. Before long, people looking in the store's big front window noticed me working and began stopping in to visit. Many asked whether I would sell them a carousel horse, but because of the time it takes to carve each animal, most people couldn't afford the price. The only solution seemed to be to teach them how to carve their own animals.

Most of my students had no previous art experience and had never carved anything. I laid out a course for them that would allow anyone to understand the process of designing and carving carousel animals. Eventually, I resigned my art teaching job and devoted my entire attention to teaching carousel-animal carving. That was the beginning of Horsin' Around, and it's grown every day since.

Now people come to Horsin' Around for periods from two to four weeks, from cities such as London, Fairbanks, Los Angeles, New York, and Boston. Some seek relaxation in addition to learning how to carve their dream animal. Whatever their motivation, they all learn something extra: People who work with wood share a very special common bond.

Years ago, I was looking for some advice on carving a carousel animal, and one old fellow told me, "Just carve away everything that doesn't look like a carousel horse." Obviously, there is more to carousel-animal carving than that, yet I really feel most people can follow our instructions in this book and end up with their own hand-carved carousel animals.

Bud Ellis

A Student's Perspective

"I could never do that."
I can't count the number of times I've had someone say that to me as I stood, gouge in hand, wood chips in my hair, head bent over the big chunk of wood that would soon be my carousel horse.

Looking around at the jumble of carousel animal heads, bodies, and legs, visitors at Horsin' Around have difficulty believing owner Bud Ellis when he tells them anybody can learn to carve a carousel animal. So they ask the carvers themselves, "You mean, you really didn't know how to carve at all when you started?"

In my first days of carving at Horsin' Around, I enthusiastically answered each good-natured skeptic: "No, I really had never picked up a gouge before coming here." "Yes, I really am carving this horse myself." "No, I'm not an artist." When I could tell they were not only interested but a little envious, I'd give a little push: "I'm a writer and work only with words. If I can carve one, I know you can carve one. Just try it!"

But after talking to a steady stream of onlookers and getting no takers, I began to wonder. Could anybody who really wanted to carve a carousel animal carve one, as Bud believed? I looked around the studio one day and thought about what we, the Horsin' Around carvers, had in common. Our group that morning included a diesel mechanic, a nurse, a retired news photographer, a military veteran, a secretary, a travel agent, an engineer, and a pilot. Such a diverse gathering of people, and yet here we were, all taking time out of our busy lives to do the same crazy thing: carve a carousel animal. But lots of people wanted to own a carousel animal, and most couldn't even imagine trying to carve one themselves. What made us different?

The answer was a simple little thing called a "leap of faith." We were all carving carousel animals because Bud told us we could and we believed him. I was the classic example of that. I took two weeks off and drove almost 400 miles by myself to a city I'd never even seen to learn carving at Horsin' Around, all because I believed Bud when he sent me a few photos of animals students had carved and told me I could do it, too.

You might say leaps of faith are common at Horsin' Around. Bud made a leap when he gave up his career as an art teacher and started teaching people to carve their own animals. Then he made another one when he, his wife, Johnnie, and a handful of his faithful carvers convinced the city of Chattanooga to let them build the city a beautiful carousel of its own. Now, he and I are making a leap together by writing this book.

If you love wooden carousel animals as we do and really want to carve one yourself, the secret— as I see it—is simple:
LEAP!

Rhonda Hoeckley

A beautiful carousel horse inspired by a leap of faith!

A Word From Charles Walker

Growing up in the small town of Griffin, Georgia, in the '40s and '50s, I was always fascinated by carnivals. These traveling entertainment shows would pass through town in the fall on the way to Florida for the winter, often stopping to play fairs. They would have small two-row carousels with band organs in their units.

Once a year, our family would go to Lakewood Park in Atlanta, Georgia, to visit the Southeastern Fair and ride the beautiful Philadelphia Toboggan Co. four-row carousel. I would spend hours listening to the beautiful band organ and watching riders get on and off what, to me, was a revolving high-class art gallery. It was during these trips to the fair that I realized just how serious my love for carousels was.

While growing up, I noticed there were fewer carousels, and many of them were in disrepair. When I learned that the National Carousel Association was being started, I was eager to join and work to preserve them. I am now a carousel owner, and have enjoyed working in public entertainment.

Over the years, we have lost hundreds of carousels due to neglect, fire, and the zeal of private collectors to own their own antique carousel animal. I am happy to see organizations dedicated to carving new animals to repopulate old historic frames. Bud Ellis and the Horsin' Around group from Chattanooga, Tennessee, are to be commended for their efforts to repopulate a very old historic Dentzel machine for the city of Chattanooga. I hope that through the teachings and experience of these carvers, the almost obsolete art of carving carousel animals from wood can survive for the enjoyment of future generations.

Charles Walker

Charles Walker's involvement with carousels travels back 30 years or more when he worked to save several old carousels. He is responsible for helping start the National Carousel Association, and currently holds the title of Conservation Chairman of the NCA. Charles is an indispensable source of information for those needing advice about their carousel machines or the whereabouts of machines they recall from their youth.

INTRODUCTION

People say carousels are magical. We believe it, and you must believe it a little, too, to pick up this book and look inside. Everyone who wants to carve a carousel animal wants to capture a little of that magic for himself, and we believe that with some instruction and a little perseverance, you can do just that.

At my carousel carving school, Horsin' Around, we have discovered firsthand that almost anyone with a strong enough desire can carve any type of carousel animal. Very few of our students have had any art experience, much less any carving experience.

Our main motivation for writing this book is to get information to the typical beginner. Most how-to books on carving carousel animals have lots of photos of finished animals, but not enough information on how to actually start carving or avoid problems before they begin. This book covers those topics and more. It is different from other books on the subject in that it is written by a teacher and a student together, in the hope that looking at carousel animal carving from both perspectives will make the book more complete.

We wish we could tell you that you can carve your dream carousel animal with a few simple tools you have lying around the house, but that's just not true. If you are serious about carving a full-size animal, you will need to either borrow or buy a few power tools and a few different-sized and -shaped chisels. If you are new to carving, don't rush out and buy a full carving "set," as it might be a waste of your money. Every carver's taste in tools is different, and you're probably better off buying tools one or two at a time as you need them. In this book, we give you an idea of a few useful tools you can start with.

Obviously, you will also have to invest in wood, most probably basswood. This will cost some money, but because of our approach to carving we don't recommend that you buy all the wood (or tools) at once.

At Horsin' Around and in this book, people are instructed to start carving the head first, for several reasons. One, carving the head teaches just about everything you need to know to carve the rest of the animal. Two, the head takes a smaller amount of wood than the body (where some books suggest you start), so you don't have to buy all the wood at once to get started. And three, if after you carve the head you're unable to carve the rest of the animal, you can still proudly display the head as a worthy carving accomplishment on its own. (Trust us, displaying a headless, legless, carved horse body in your home is much less impressive.) Using this approach will help you spread out the money you have to spend on both tools and wood.

One thing you need to remember before you get started is that carousel carving is not an art that is immediately learned. It can take a few months of consistent work, or much longer if your carving time is precious and short. But don't let this frighten you away from attempting to learn how to carve. If you keep at it, one day you will finish your dream animal.

In our approach to carving carousel animals, the head is the first area to be carved.

PART ONE

Preparing for Your First Carousel Carving

The organ is playing, the lights are twinkling, the animals are spinning by. There goes a horse with flowers, and a soldier's horse, and an Indian pony...and a tiger stalking its prey! Look, there's a zebra, and a bear, and—is that a cat with a fish in its mouth? There it is again! Suddenly, the spinning starts to slow. It's time to choose an animal to ride!

Which one do you choose to carve? There are so many wonderful animals to choose, from horses to wild animals to sea serpents, in different styles and different poses. In this book, we don't focus on carving one particular animal, but instead teach you how to approach the carving of any carousel animal. You get to decide whether you want to carve a replica of an antique animal, combine elements of several antique animals, or even design an animal of your own. The possibilities are limited only by your own taste and creativity.

Fortunately, choosing the animal you want to carve differs in one important way from choosing the animal you want to ride: They're both exciting, but when carving you don't have to beat out the big kid to get the animal you want.

1

Choosing the Animal You Want to Carve

As with any big project, the work you do in the beginning plays an important part in its ultimate success. Carving a carousel animal is a big endeavor, so you need to give your choice of animal the thought and preparation it deserves.

The first step to choosing your animal is learning as much as you can about carousels and the people who manufactured the machines and carved the animals. The best way to do this is to conduct a bit of old-fashioned research. A handful of excellent books have been written about carousel art, and most of them are filled with wonderful color photographs. If you visit the library or bookstore and look up books with the words "carousel," "painted ponies," "fairground art," and "merry-go-round" in their titles, you should find most of them. While reading, look specifically for information on the different styles of animals, and watch for good photographs of antique carousel animals. (Later, if you make your own pattern, you'll need a photograph of the animal you choose to make your blueprint.)

Though the photographs will make you want to page through the books quickly to see the next incredible animal, you should spend some time reading the information. Carving a full-size carousel animal costs you both time and money, and you don't want to get partway into the process and suddenly wish you'd chosen another animal, or a different carver's style to emulate. Do your homework up front, and you'll be happier with the results.

As you're reading, it will help to be familiar with a few basic carousel terms:

JUMPER—A carousel animal that is jumping, and thus has all four feet off the platform. Jumpers move up and down as the carousel turns.

LEAD HORSE—The fanciest horse on the outside row of the machine. The operator used the lead horse to help keep track of the revolutions of the carousel.

MENAGERIE FIGURE—A carousel animal that is something other than a horse.

PRANCER—A carousel animal that has its front legs raised and its back feet on the platform. It is stationary on the carousel.

ROMANCE SIDE—The side of the animal that faces the spectators (the right side on American carousels, and the left side on English machines). The romance side is usually more elaborately carved than the other side.

SIDE FIGURE—A carved figure on or near the front shoulder of the romance side of an animal. It is sometimes called "Cherni figure," so-named for the carver Salvatore Cernigliaro, who carved some of the most elaborate side figures.

STANDER—A carousel animal with at least three feet touching the platform. It is stationary on the carousel.

TRAPPINGS—The equipment and coverings or decorations of an animal. Some of the more distinctive trappings include "armored" (medieval armor) and "military" (realistic military equipment) trappings.

CAROUSEL ANIMAL STYLES

In the books, you will learn that the era of hand-carved carousels in America began in the late 1860s, when the first European master carvers emigrated to America and began carving carousels for their new country's amusement pleasure. Most of these carvers learned their skills in their home countries by making furniture and building wooden ships. The freedom they found in America fueled their creativity, and they carved some exciting carousel animals that were much more ornate and varied than those on the European carousels.

The "golden age" of carousels was the period between 1905 and 1925, when the industry was booming and many carousels full of elaborately carved animals were being produced. Carousels you may remember riding as a child were perhaps produced during this period, as were some of the most famous carousel carvings. Since carousels seem to be such a vivid image from our past, you might be surprised to learn that the whole carousel era did not last very long. Historians consider it to have ended in the early 1930s, brought down in part by the Depression.

The most well-known carousel carvings can more or less be categorized as one of three different styles: the Philadelphia style, the Coney Island style, and the County (or Country) Fair style. The Philadelphia style is characterized by very realistic-looking horses and other animals in natural poses. It was the style of famous carvers such as Gustav Dentzel, Daniel Muller, and Salvatore Cernigliaro. The Coney Island style features flashy animals with dramatic details, such as flying or tumbling gold-leaf manes and fanciful trappings. Some of the Coney-Island-style carvers included Marcus Illions, Charles Looff, Charles Carmel, John Zalar, and the team of Solomon Stein and Harry Goldstein.

The third style, the County Fair style, is the one seen in the traveling carnivals. It is characterized by strong, functional animals, often simply carved (and thus less realistic) so they would hold up under the abuse of constant transport. The County Fair style is known more for its manufacturers—including Charles Dare, Charles W. Parker, and the Herschell and Spillman families—than its carvers. Illus. 1-1 to 1-7 are drawings representing the three styles.

As you read about the different carousel makers and carvers and look at the photographs of the old carvings, you'll most likely find that you are drawn to a particular style, or even a particular carver. It has been our experience at Horsin' Around that many people already have some idea of what style of animal they would like to carve, based on childhood memories of riding the carousel in their neighborhood. Looking at these books might make you remember a favorite carousel, as well.

Once you've done your homework and know the style you like, you next want to consider the animal's size and complexity.

ANIMAL SIZE AND COMPLEXITY

Choosing the size of the animal you will carve is purely personal. A small animal is a good size for a child's room, since it doesn't take up as much space and most young people are so happy to get one they don't care how big it is. We've never liked carving carousel animals at one-third-size or smaller, however; after working with so many big animals, somehow it doesn't feel like the real thing to us unless it's full size. But some people don't have room for the bigger animals, and you need to be practical.

If you want to make your carousel animal true to the original size, you need to know a few facts. Carousels usually had one to four rows of animals (although a few had five or six rows).The outer row animals were larger than the inner row animals. Sizes for the different row animals varied among both manufacturers and individual machines.

You can find information on the dimensions of specific antique carousel animals in several of the carousel history books. However, following are approximate dimensions for length for large, medium, and small animals that are based on measurements taken from an antique Dentzel machine. (Note: These measurements are for the body only. Add about 20 to 30 percent for head and tail to estimate total length.)

Large Animal (outer row): 46-inch body

Medium-Size Animal (second row): 35- to 36-inch body

Small Animal (inner-row jumper): 31-inch body

The complexity of the animal you choose is also a matter of choice. Some of the antique animals were very ornate, and some were relatively simple yet elegant. If you want a rewarding challenge, we suggest you carve the one you really love. Don't let the complexity of the carving scare you; more ornate animals just take longer to do.

DECIDING BETWEEN A HORSE AND A MENAGERIE ANIMAL

Most carvers pick some style of horse for their first carving, but it does not necessarily take any more or less time to carve a menagerie animal. Menagerie animals on carousels included lions, tigers, zebras, rabbits, camels, ostriches, bears, goats, sea serpents, cats, dogs, pigs, roosters, and more. Some of the menagerie animals are not as complicated as most horses, and some are more involved. Interestingly, most of our students usually carve something besides a horse for their second animal. Each animal presents its own set of problems and pleasures as the carving unfolds, so don't feel that you have to choose a horse if you really want to carve a different animal.

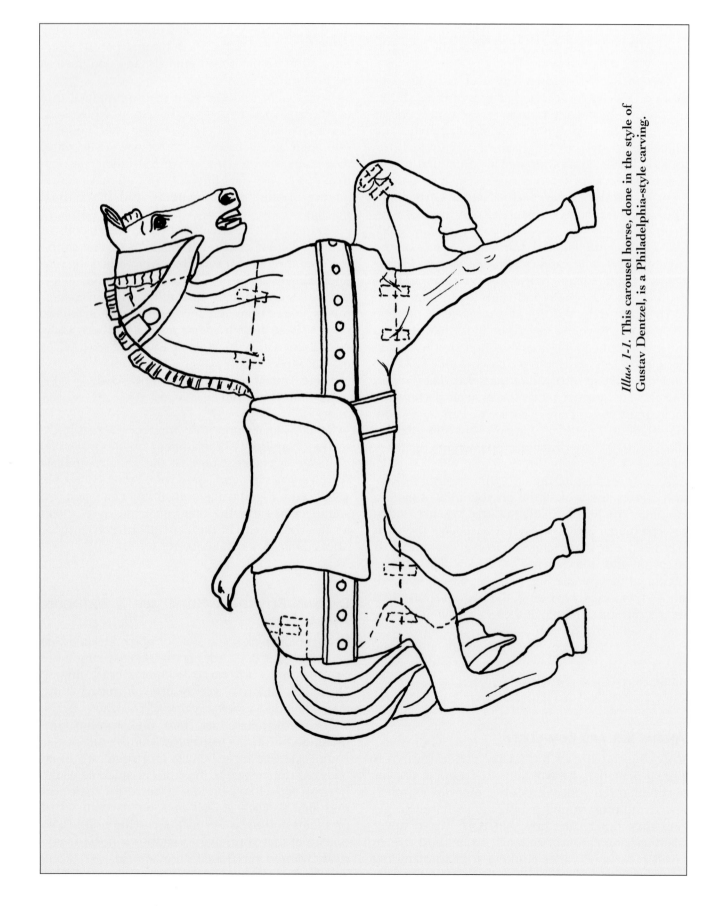

Illus. 1-1. This carousel horse, done in the style of Gustav Dentzel, is a Philadelphia-style carving.

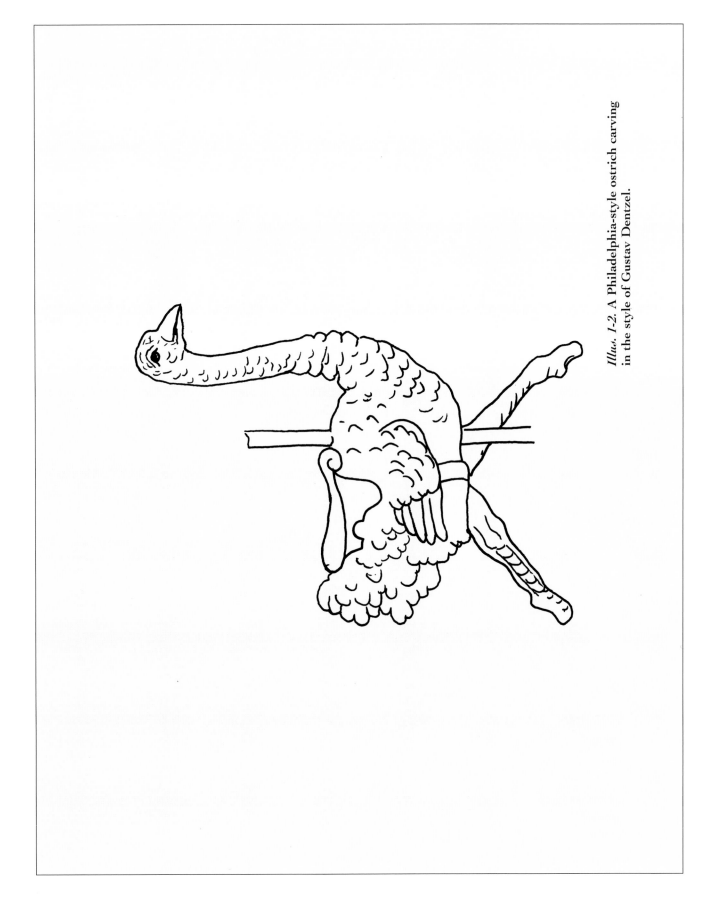

Illus. 1-2. A Philadelphia-style ostrich carving in the style of Gustav Dentzel.

Illus. 1-3. This carousel horse, done in the John Zalar style, is categorized as a Coney-Island-style carving.

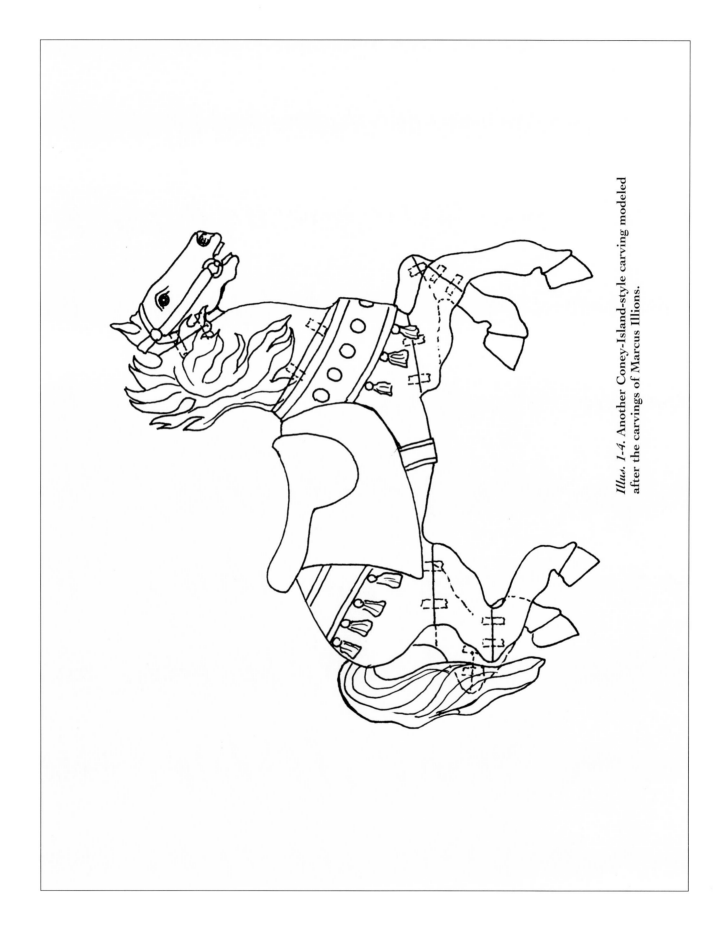

Illus. 1-4. Another Coney-Island-style carving modeled after the carvings of Marcus Illions.

Illus. 1-5. This Herschell–Spillman zebra falls under the category of County Fair style.

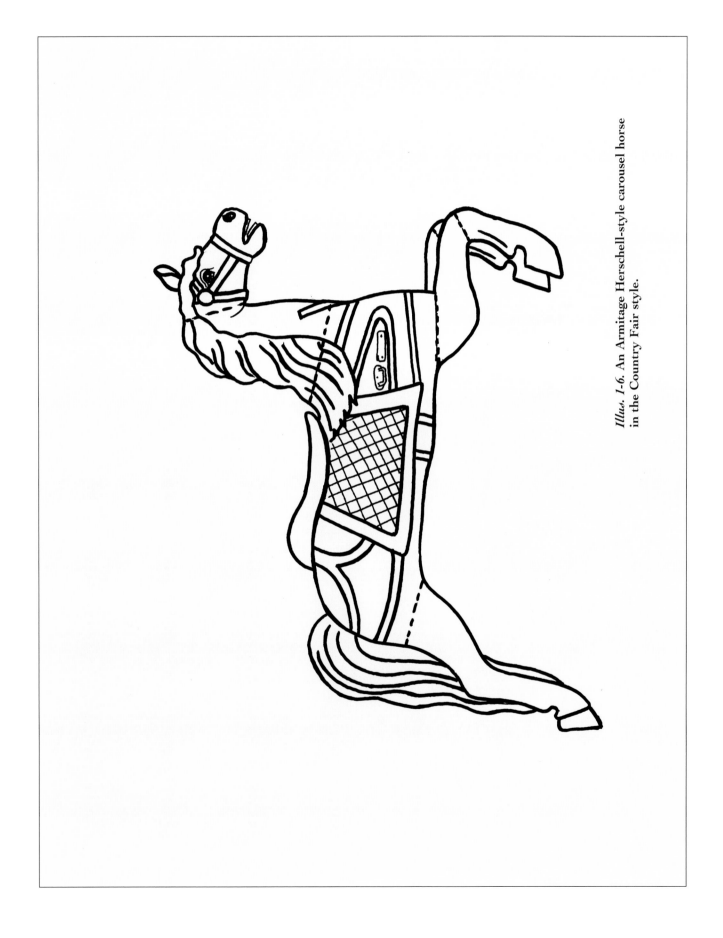

Illus. 1-6. An Armitage Herschell-style carousel horse in the Country Fair style.

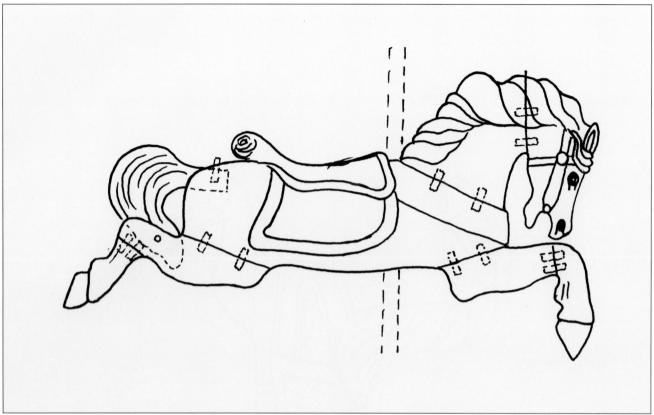

Illus. 1-7. **Another County-Fair-style carousel horse done in the style of C.W. Parker.**

FINDING A GOOD PHOTOGRAPH OR DRAWING

Once you have determined the type of carousel animal you'd like to carve and its size and complexity, go through the books again and look at all the photographs and drawings of carousel animals you can find that fit your preferences. Also, look at the patterns we provide in Chapter 4, and if you're lucky enough to have a real carousel near you, look at that, too. If you find an animal that you really love, you can carve a replica of that same animal. If you find several you like, you can combine features of each (such as the head from one and the trappings from another, if they are compatible) to make your own design. If you're an artist, you can design your own animal from scratch.

Most first-time carvers fall in love with one of the antique horses and carve a replica (Illus. 1-8). To do this, you need to find a pattern (such as those provided in Chapter 4) or a good side-view photograph of the full animal which you can use to make your blueprint. If you plan to combine features of several antique animals, try to find good side-view photos of each animal. If you want to carve one you've seen on a real carousel, take several side-view photographs of the full animal, as well as many photos of the animal at all different angles. If you plan to design your own animal from scratch, draw a detailed scale drawing.

Once you've chosen your animal, get ready to begin an experience you'll never forget. Keep in mind, once again, that it takes time to carve a carousel animal. The best advice we can give you is to enjoy every day you get to carve, and not worry about the time. It's not a race, and when you finish you'll probably want to start another animal (Illus. 1-9). Many people do.

Illus. 1-8. A replica of an antique horse.

Illus. 1-9. A carver at Horsin' Around works as a finished horse looks on.

2
Tools and Materials

We could call this chapter the "nuts and bolts" chapter, except that in this book we teach you how to build and carve carousel animals like the master carvers at the turn of the century did—without nuts or bolts or any metal pieces, save the pole. Building and carving your animal does require that you use some specific tools and materials, however, and this chapter gives you a basic overview of what you'll need.

To explain what you will need, it's necessary to refer to certain steps of the process. Don't worry if you don't completely understand those steps at this point. They are described in more detail in later chapters when you need to perform them.

TOOLS

Though you could go out and spend a fortune on carving tools, there is no need to do so. Just a few tools, as described below, are enough to get the job done.

Chisels and Gouges, and Other Hand Tools

A chisel is a metal tool with a wooden handle and a cutting edge at the end of its shaft. You will use a few flat-tipped chisels to carve your animal, but mostly you will use a type of chisel called a gouge, which has a curved blade (Illus. 2-1).

Illus. 2-1. **This carver is using a large gouge and mallet.**

Gouges and chisels come in different blade widths. Gouges also come in different degrees of blade curve (called sweep) to remove greater or lesser amounts of wood.

There are three different types of gouges besides the basic gouge that are useful when carving a carousel animal. The V-parting tool is straight-sided with a V-shaped bottom edge. It is used for outlining, adding detail, and undercutting. A veiner is more of a U-shaped gouge, and is useful in outlining relief work and in carving the mane and tail. A spoon gouge is shaped similar to an everyday spoon. It is useful for digging out relatively deep holes, such as in the ear or nostril. It is not essential that you own a spoon gouge.

You can use a mallet—the wood-carver's hammer—to drive both chisels and gouges, or you can use your hands. We have discovered that using a heavier mallet (especially a rubber-coated one) really removes excess wood quickly without tiring the arm. Conversely, using a wood or rubber-coated lighter mallet will very quickly wear down even the most enthusiastic carver. Mallets are discussed further in Chapter 5, Carving Techniques.

For the person "roughing out" or carving the rough shape of his first horse or animal, a No. 5 sweep gouge about 35 millimeters wide or wider is a good tool to start with. At Horsin' Around, where we have many students carving at once, we use a right-angle grinder with a special chain-saw cutting blade mounted on it (Illus. 2-2) to rough out the general shape of the animals. This is a much faster method of roughing out. However, this tool should only be used by the experienced carver or woodworker who has used power tools.

Once you have removed most of the excess wood and your animal is closer to its final shape, you will have to start carving a finer shape to find the animal in the wood. We have found that with the following tools, you can do just about everything:

20-mm #5 sweep gouge (medium gouge, shallow sweep)

Illus. 2-2. **Roughing out an animal using a right-angle grinder with a chain-saw blade attachment.**

13-mm #9 sweep gouge (medium gouge, medium sweep)

10-mm #11 sweep gouge (medium veiner)

14-mm #12 sweep V-parting tool (medium V-tool)

When you reach the final-detail stage of your carving, these tools would be helpful:

7-mm #9 sweep gouge (small gouge, medium sweep)

8-mm #7 sweep gouge (small gouge, shallow sweep)

8-mm #12 sweep V-parting tool (small V-tool)
Micro-carving set (very small gouges for very fine detail work)

Another useful tool for your project is a riffler file, a small shaped file that can help you shape wood. You will also find that 3/4-inch metal dowel centers are very handy. These inexpensive spike-tipped marking aids help you mark where a matching hole should be drilled when pegging (inserting wooden dowel pegs) into joints to make them stronger.

If you are unfamiliar with carving tools, you might want to visit your local woodworking store, contact your local wood-carving club, or borrow a woodworking catalog to take a look at chisels, gouges, and mallets.

Sharpening Your Chisels

Keeping your chisels sharp will save you time when woodworking. It also keeps you from injuring yourself, since a blunt tool is not a safe tool. Most new chisels are sharpened at the factory, but after several hours of use they will need resharpening. We recommend using a combination sharpening stone with fine grit on one side and coarse grit on the other. We also recommend using what's called a slipstone to remove small burrs from the inside of the chisel's sweep and off the backside of its cutting edge. If you've never sharpened a tool before, a basic sharpening book from your local library or bookstore can show you how, as can members of your local wood-carving club. Sharp tools are very important, so it's worth your time to learn to do it right.

With our volume of students at Horsin' Around, sharpening by hand has proven to be too slow. If you find you love to carve, you might want to invest in a sharpening system such as we did. The one we use does not burn up tools and never seems to break down. Our system (Illus. 2-3 and 2-4) is composed of bench grinders with three wheels: one covered with rough sandpaper, one covered with fine sandpaper, and one covered with a leather belt for stropping the final sharpness. These systems and others are available for sale in woodworking catalogs.

However you sharpen your tools, it's important to store them in such a way that the blades can't knock against each other, since this will dull or nick them. Many carvers keep their tools in cloth rolls that have a pocket for each tool. These are also available for sale in woodworking catalogs.

Useful Power Tools for Sawing, Carving, and Sanding

There are several power tools that are either necessary or very useful when you are cutting out

Illus. 2-3. **A carver sharpening her tools with a sharpening system.**

your pieces and roughing out your animal. Their usefulness is brief, however, so you might not want to buy them if you can borrow them or find a woodworking shop you can use (such as those provided at colleges, military bases, or city recreation facilities). Be advised that it's a good idea to wear a dust mask when using the tools, however, since inhaling large amounts of wood dust over time can be toxic.

Illus. 2-4. **A close-up look at the sharpening system at Horsin' Around.**

Illus. 2-5. **A carver using a radial arm saw.**

Table Saw or Radial Arm Saw—These saws (Illus. 2-5) are used to cut your new lumber into manageable pieces that can then fit in the bandsaw. If you do not own one and your budget doesn't allow buying one (they can be expensive), a simple hand-held circular saw or even a handsaw will do.

Band saw—It's just about impossible to build a large carousel horse for carving without a band saw (Illus. 2-6). After you have traced your pattern pieces on your wood, you will need the band saw to cut out the many pieces (many of which are intricately curved) that you will laminate to make what's called your animal blank.

Planer—If you are carving several animals or do other carving projects, a thickness planer (which "surfaces" or levels the wood) will save you lots of money. However, planers take time to use and make large messes. Horsin' Around has more than 50 animals being carved at one time in the shop, so we find it easier and faster to order our wood already planed. You will probably want to do the same. We do, however, use an inexpensive hand planer to surface areas that are to be glued together.

Jointer—A jointer (Illus. 2-7) is not a tool that you use every day, but it's really handy in cleaning up and smoothing the edges of boards. Once again, however, we have the lumber company do this for us, to save the floor space a jointer takes up.

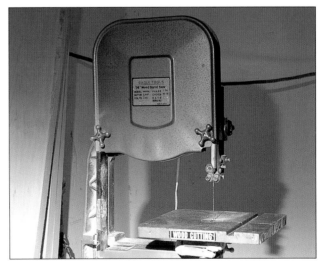

Illus. 2-6. **A large band saw that is used at Horsin' Around.**

Belt/Disc Floor-Model Sander—This combination belt and disc sander (Illus. 2-8) can be used to achieve consistent, smooth surfaces on the flat

Illus. 2-7. **A jointer is used to smooth edges of boards.**

Illus. 2-8. **A belt/disc floor-model sander.**

areas of the leg parts which have to be glued together to make a whole leg, and the surfaces where the head joins the top of the neck and the neck joins the body. You can also use a hand-held belt sander, but you don't get as smooth a surface.

Electric Drill—Most carvers have at least one electric drill. This tool is helpful for both drilling holes for the pegs that help hold your animal together, and for sanding. If you are considering using or buying an electric drill, you should be able to buy the attachments you need at any hardware store. If you decide to purchase one, you should buy one that has both a low and a high speed. Drill bits cut much better at a low speed, whereas sanding with a drill is more effective at a higher speed.

Dremel Tool—This hand-held power tool can be used for some detail power carving, but is really invaluable for sanding. It can be fitted with small sanding drums or a larger piece of hand-cut sandpaper and used to quickly sand areas that would take you much longer by hand.

Power-Tool Safety Instructions

Always observe the following precautions when using power tools:

1. Before using any power tool, read and understand its operations manual. A good manual will describe proper techniques and procedures.

2. Think through each procedure before you do it. If you feel it is potentially dangerous, find another way to accomplish the same result.

3. Keep the blades on your power tools and your chisels and gouges sharp and maintain them prop-

erly. Dull tools are potentially dangerous because you have to exert extra pressure when you cut. Therefore, you are more likely to slip and get your hands in the way of the cutting edge.

4. Wear the proper safety equipment. Always wear safety glasses or goggles. Also wear a face shield when using a tool that produces lots of chips. As mentioned earlier, wear a dust mask whenever you're sanding or doing operations that produce lots of dust. If there is a dust collector available for the tool, always use it.

5. Don't wear loose clothing when working. Keep your sleeves rolled up. Remember that anything loose can be pulled into a blade if it gets caught. Don't wear any type of jewelry.

6. Never attempt to adjust any power tool while it is plugged in or has its battery in place.

7. Do not do any woodworking if you have taken drugs or alcohol. Some medications can cause drowsiness and other effects that make it dangerous to use woodworking tools, so read their labels and follow your doctor's advice.

MATERIALS
Finding and Storing Good Wood

The original carousel animals were carved from almost any wood readily available to the carver. For these projects, however, we highly recommend using basswood (Illus. 2-9), the wood many of the master carvers used. It is classified as a soft hardwood, because it is soft and has a fine texture, which makes it carve easily.

We use basswood almost exclusively at Horsin' Around, and it has been our experience that it has a very even, smooth grain and seldom has knot-holes or bad areas. Basswood is sometimes called limewood or linden.

Many lumber companies carry basswood or can get it quickly. We buy 2-inch-thick boards, and laminate them (by gluing layers together) to make our pieces. Most lumber companies still carry 1-inch-thick basswood for cabinetmakers. This can be laminated as well, but will involve more layers and thus more work.

Certain areas of the country do not have bass-wood available. If you live in one of these areas, you might try using soft heart pine or a good sugar pine or poplar.

Once you've located a good source of basswood, you must keep it in a dry storage area. When ordering this wood, specify that it be kiln-dried and planed. (We also ask the lumber company to have one edge joined, if possible.) When not kiln-dried, basswood (like most other woods) will soak up moisture when left outside or when left to sit inside for long periods without being painted. We have discovered that basswood will crack at glue joints when moisture has warped the boards.

Determining the Amount of Wood to Order

Obviously, how much wood you need to order depends on the animal you are carving. For example, a big lion head with a wild mane takes more wood than a horse head with a very tame mane. At Horsin' Around, we use the following rough estimates when ordering our wood. (Note: These estimates are generous. We have included a separate estimate for wood for the head only, since we recommend that people start by ordering just the wood for the head until they know whether they want to continue to carve the rest of the animal.)

Large animal: 120 board feet for the entire animal, 40 board feet for just the head.

Medium animal: 100 board feet for the entire animal, 30 board feet for just the head.

Small animal: 90 board feet for the entire animal, 30 board feet for just the head.

Gluing and Clamping the Pieces

After the pieces have been cut out with the band saw, their edges have been sanded, and sawdust has been dusted off the pieces, they have to be laminated. After trying several types of glues, we discovered that the plain yellow wood glue avail-able at any hardware store or discount store does a really good job of gluing the pieces together to make the parts of the carving blank.

When you reach the gluing phase, you will also need clamps. Wood and iron clamps can be purchased in large hardware stores or from wood-working stores and magazines. Very often, we've seen the wooden ones in flea markets at reduced prices, so keep your eyes open if you like to browse at flea markets.

We use hand-screw clamps to hold the pieces of the legs and head together as they dry. After gluing the legs, you can clamp together several sets of legs with just two sets of pipe clamps. We use at least six pipe clamps (about 36 inches long) when gluing together the pieces of the body (Illus. 2-10). We also use band clamps, which consist of a nylon web band and a ratchet mechanism to tighten it.

Illus. 2-9. **Planks of basswood ready to be cut into pieces.**

Illus. 2-10. **Pipe clamps holding together a glued-up body as it dries.**

Illus. 2-11. **A carver gluing up parts of a carousel animal.**

If you can't buy or borrow the larger clamps to clamp the big pieces, you might try using a method ship carvers used when gluing up big wood chunks. First, lash up the piece with strong rope, and then pound in thin wedges of waste wood under the rope to make the binding tight.

There are a couple of tips you should know about gluing and clamping the pieces (Illus. 2-11). First, always coat both surfaces with glue. After you clamp, have some old rags handy to mop up the glue that squeezes out of the joint. If you let the glue drips dry on the wood, they will quickly dull your tools later when you have to carve them off. Also, let the wood sit for about five minutes before clamping it, so the glue has a chance to start setting. And remember not to put too much pressure on the joints when you clamp your pieces, or you will squeeze out all the glue.

A quick note about the clamps: You can try to borrow clamps for the gluing process if you'd rather not buy them, but bear in mind that you will need clamps or a vise later when you start carving (Illus. 2-12). The different pieces of your horse must be secured to a steady surface before you can safely carve them.

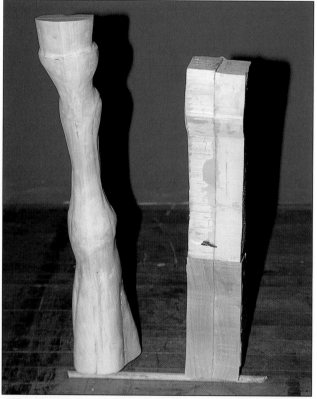

Illus. 2-12. **A carved leg (at left) compared to a leg blank.**

3

Making Your Blueprint

Once you've chosen the animal you want to carve and gathered your tools and materials, the next step is to make your full-size blueprint. The blueprint will be cut apart to make patterns used to trace and cut out the wood pieces you will laminate to make your carving blank.

You can make a blueprint from a good side-view photograph of the entire animal, from a pattern (such as those we provide in Chapter 4), or from an original-scale drawing. To draw the blueprint, you will need a very large piece of paper (as shown in Illus. 3-1). We've found that a quick trip to your local newspaper office can give you ample supplies of blank newsprint, which works great. Most newspaper offices have small ends of rolls left, and are more than happy to give you or sell you enough for several horses.

When you get your paper, get a generous amount. Some people like to make an extra blueprint, so they have a complete one to refer to throughout the carving process or to keep as a souvenir of their first carving. Even if you make just one blueprint of the whole animal, you'll need to make a second blueprint of at least the head and neck area, to help when you're carving those parts.

Before you enlarge your photo or pattern to make the blueprint, you have to mark the pattern cutting lines. Follow the example in Illus. 3-2 to mark your pattern.

COPYING METHODS

If you're starting your first animal and you're not an exceptionally talented artist, it's probably wise to use a copying techique to make your blueprint. It's very difficult to draw a horse and have it look realistic, so don't feel that you must spend hours drawing your own full-size blueprint freehand. Carving something this complicated is difficult enough, so give yourself a break at this stage.

We've learned that if you're using a photograph to make your blueprint, using only good side-view shots will eliminate many camera and angle

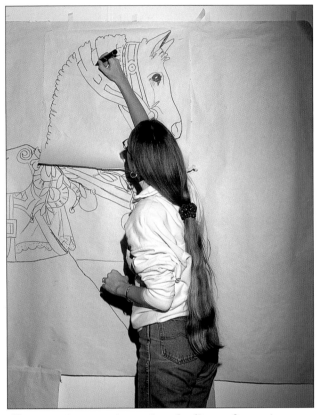

Illus. 3-1. **A carver is tracing the lines of a project photo to make a blueprint.**

distortion problems. But even if you use a side-view photograph, one obvious camera distortion will remain: The legs on the far side of the horse will appear shorter than the legs on the near side of the horse. Since you need all the legs to be the same length so your animal can stand properly, this distortion must be corrected. To compensate for this, see the section on camera distortion later in this chapter.

We suggest you use one of two copying methods to make your blueprint. The two methods, the grid and the projection methods, are described below.

The Grid Method

The grid method involves converting the photograph or pattern of your animal into a small grid,

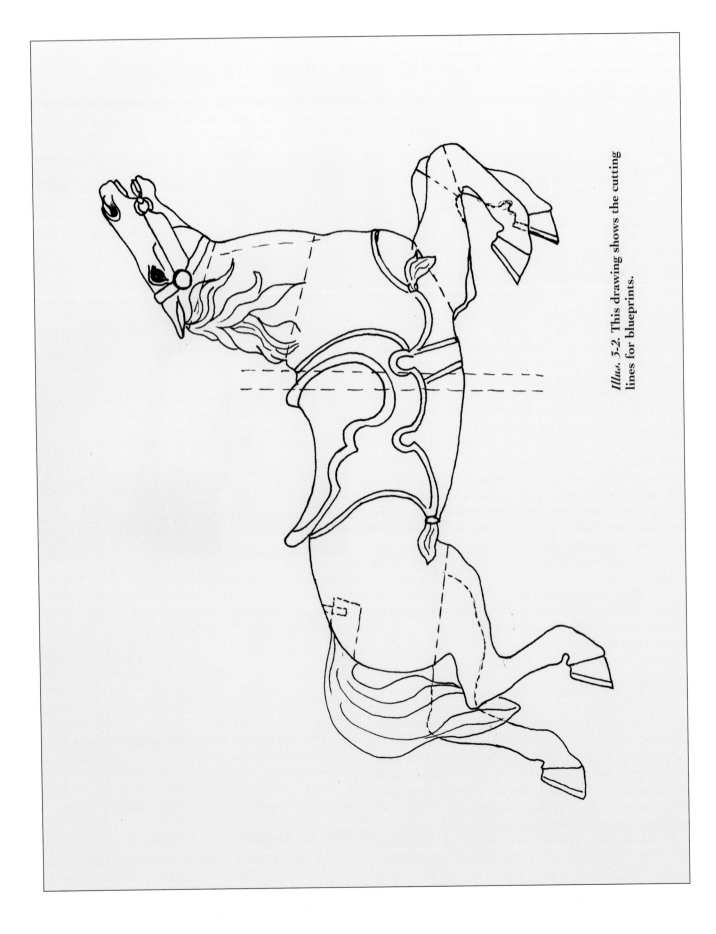

Illus. 3-2. This drawing shows the cutting lines for blueprints.

and then enlarging each square manually on a larger sheet of paper to meet the specified size of your carving. We've found that enlarging drawings from a 1/2-inch square to a 4-inch-square grid is an easy scale to work with, but any scale will work.

First, find a pattern or photo of your chosen antique carousel animal or a drawing of the animal you like. Cover the illustration with an 8½ x 11-inch piece of clear acetate (commonly found in office supply stores for use with overhead projectors), and trace the lines of your pattern or photo on the acetate with a fine felt-tip marker. Pay close attention to detail while tracing.

Next, using a ruler, make your grid on a piece of paper the same size as the acetate. Tape your gridded paper to the back of your acetate tracing. (You can use engineering paper if it suits your grid size.) Then, using a yardstick, draw your corresponding larger grid on a piece of newsprint or similar paper which is a little larger than the finished dimensions of your carving. Finally, manually transfer the drawing, square by square, from the small grid to the large grid to make your full-size blueprint. An example of a gridded drawing is shown in Illus. 3-3.

If you're having trouble deciding on your scale, measure the distance between two critical points (such as the distance from the nose to the tail, bottom of the shoe to the top of the ear, or the bottom of the shoe to the top of the saddle), and then convert this measurement to the appropriate scale dimension. For example, if the nose-to-tail distance in the finished animal will be 50 inches, and the nose-to-tail distance in your tracing is 5 inches, then divide 50 by 5 to get a scale of 10. In other words, your full-size blueprint will be 10 times bigger than your tracing. If your small grid is made of 1/2-inch squares, then multiply that by 10 to get your larger grid squares of 5 inches.

The Projection Method

At Horsin' Around, we've found that the fastest and easiest method of making a full-size blueprint is to use an overhead or opaque projector (Illus. 3-4 and 3-5). To do this, first find a pattern or photo of your favorite antique carousel animal or a drawing of the animal you like. Cover the picture with an 8½ x 11-inch piece of clear acetate, and trace the lines of your picture with a fine felt-

tip marker. Pay close attention to detail while tracing.

Once you have your tracing, use the overhead projector to project it onto a large sheet of paper hung on the wall. Adjust the projector to make the image the length that you want (more about carousel animal sizes below). Then trace the lines of the projected image onto the large paper blueprint.

Don't rush out and buy an overhead projector to use the projection method. A call to one of your teacher friends can most likely help you arrange to either borrow a projector or go to the school to use one for the 10 minutes it takes to make your blueprint drawing.

Camera Distortion

To compensate for the camera distortion discussed above in which the legs on the far side of the horse appear shorter than the legs on the near side of the horse, draw a baseline along the bottom under the hoofs or feet as shown in Illus. 3-6. If you're using the overhead projector method, lower your acetate on the projector until the hoof reaches the line, and trace the missing line. We usually draw and redraw this leg in pencil until it looks natural, and then draw over the pencil marks with marker. If you are using the grid method, move the squares with the hoof and lower leg on them down to the baseline. Then fill in the missing lines by hand.

Finished Size

A quick reminder about the finished size of your carving: If you want to make your carousel animal true to the original size, you need to do some research on the sizes of carousel animals or review the approximate dimensions presented in Chapter 1. A weekend trip to a nearby carousel could provide easy measurements between rides, and be a lot of fun as well. You can also find information on the dimensions of specific antique carousel animals in a number of carousel history books.

Using Premade Patterns

In Chapter 4, we provide 33 patterns you can use for your carving, if one of the many animals strikes your fancy. Horsin' Around and several other companies and individuals sell similar patterns, as well as full-size blueprints. Some of them are well done and can produce good results. One carousel pub-

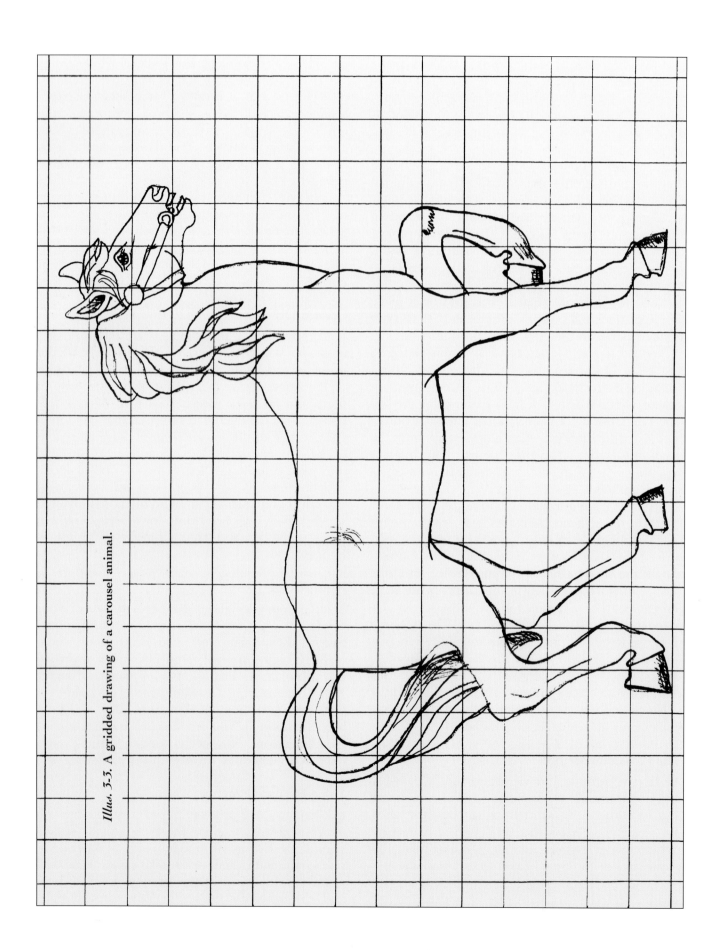

Illus. 3-3. A gridded drawing of a carousel animal.

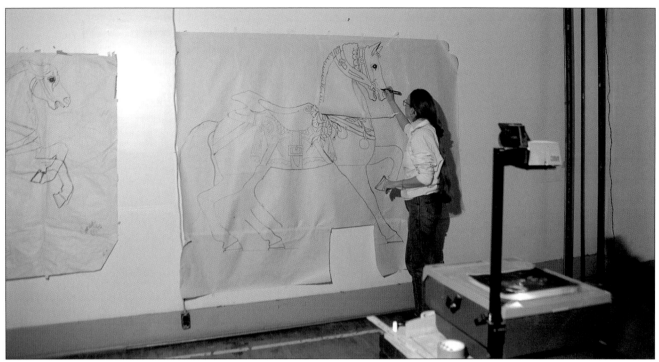

Illus. 3-4. Here a carver is using an overhead projector to project a photograph onto paper in order to trace lines onto the blueprint.

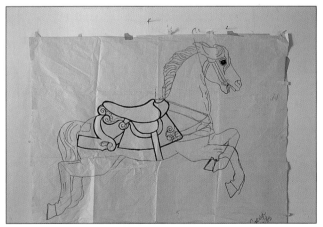

Illus. 3-5. A close-up of the drawing on the blueprint.

Illus. 3-6. Draw a baseline along the bottom of the drawing of the horse under its hoofs or feet to compensate for the camera distortion of its legs.

lication, *The Carousel News and Trader* (listed in Chapter 17), offers one side-view pattern of a carousel animal each month. These patterns are drawn by the same artist who drew the patterns in Chapter 4.

Customizing Your Animal's Saddle and Trappings

After making the basic blueprint, we usually stand back, look for distortion problems, and decide if the animal we've chosen is really the one we want to carve. This is a good time to make changes, such as adding flowers or a clinging angel, or that special saddle you like on some other horse.

If you really like a particular animal, but prefer the saddle and trappings you saw on a different animal, it's easy to customize your animal to look the way you want. One simple technique is to place an 8½ x 11-inch piece of acetate over another animal, trace its saddle, put the tracing on the overhead projector and project it onto the full-size blueprint of your own animalís body, afterward tracing it on. This idea can be used for all decorations. Obviously, the two animals need to be of similar styles and body position for this to work for larger trappings.

4

Patterns

If you followed our advice in Chapter 1 and spent some time looking through the carousel history books, you'll recognize some of the animals in the following patterns. The 30 horses and 3 menagerie animals represent a wide variety of styles and carving. If you choose to use one of these patterns for your carving project, finding a photograph of the animal or a very similar animal would still be helpful. You want as much visual information as possible to look at when you're carving. Refer to Chapter 3 for instructions on how to use these patterns to make your blueprint. The patterns are marked with a grid pattern for the benefit of those people who prefer to use the grid method of enlargement.

The following patterns were drawn by Kathleen Bond, of K.B. Leather Art.

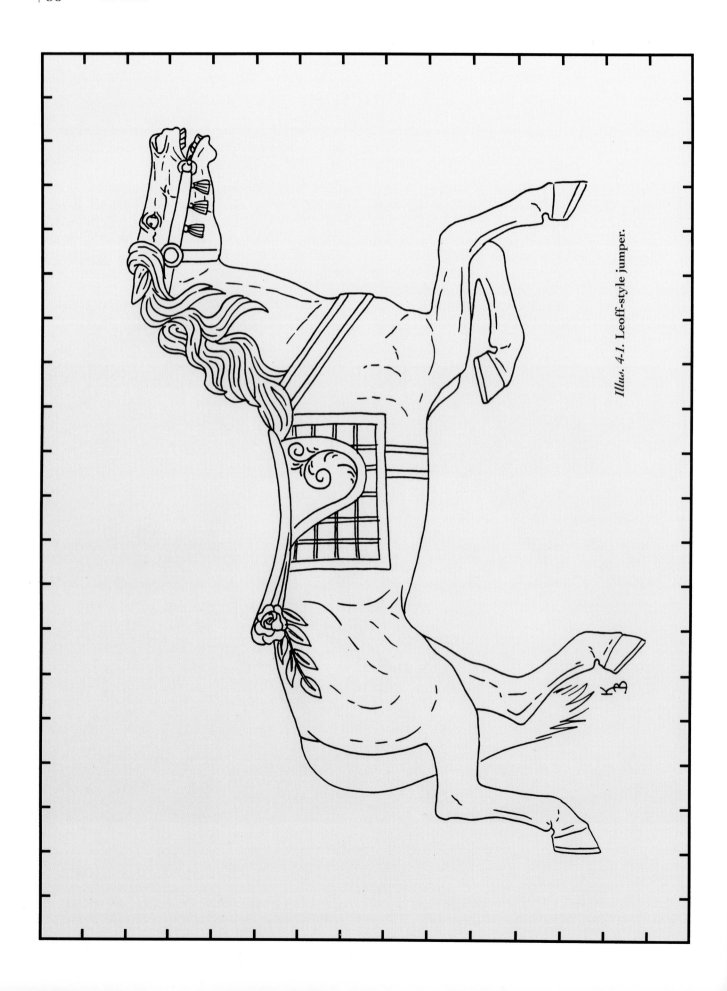

Illus. 4-1. Leoff-style jumper.

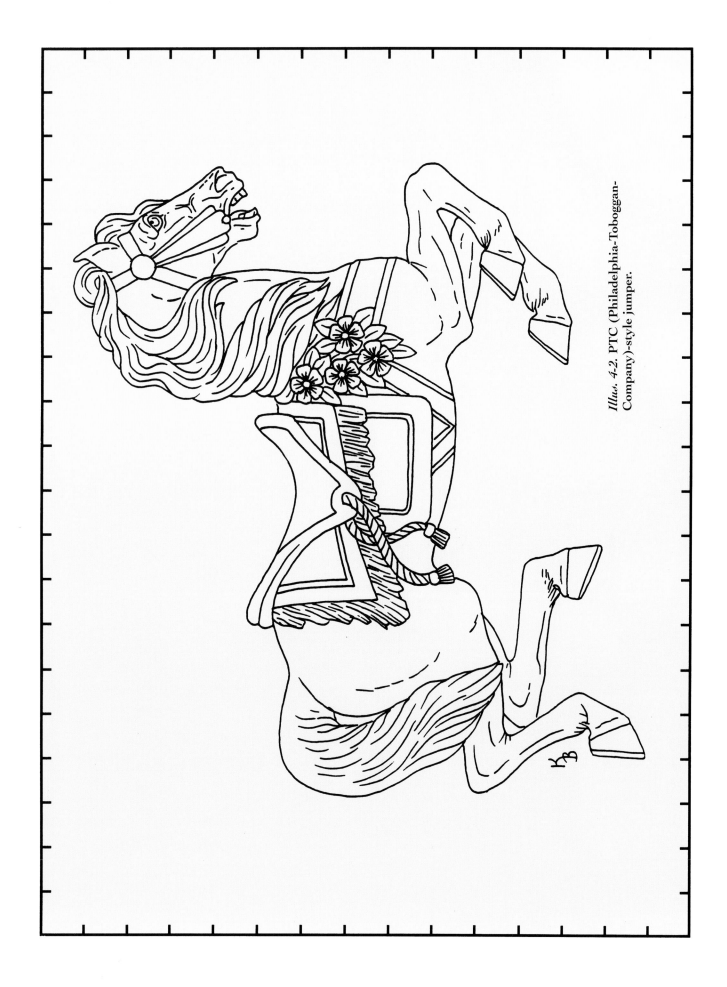

Illus. 4-2. PTC (Philadelphia-Toboggan-Company)-style jumper.

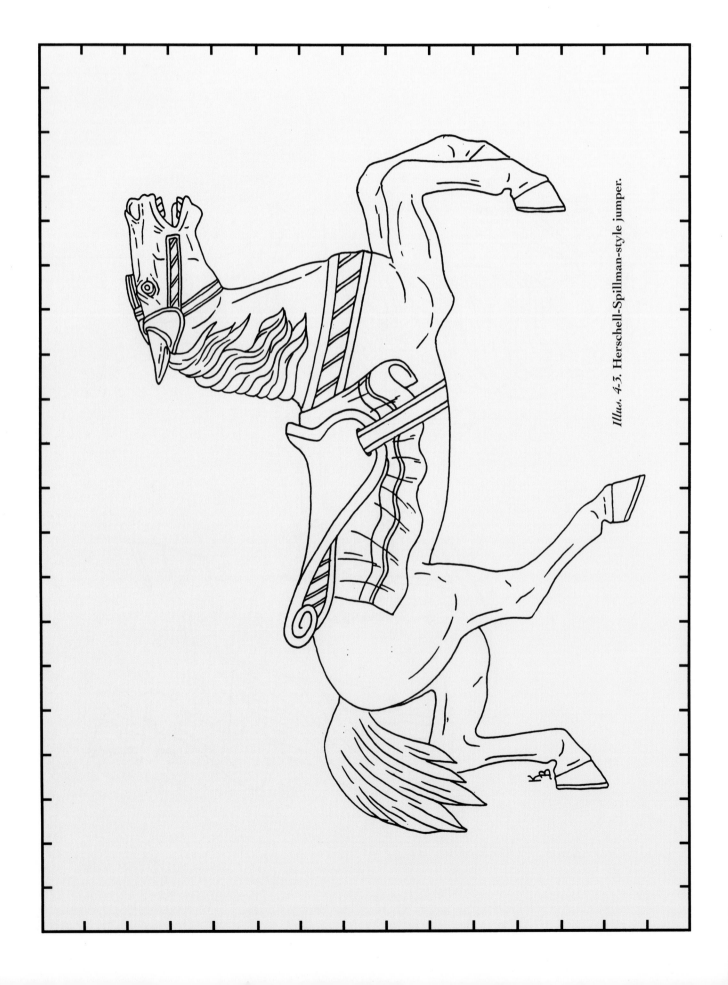

Illus. 4-3. Herschell-Spillman-style jumper.

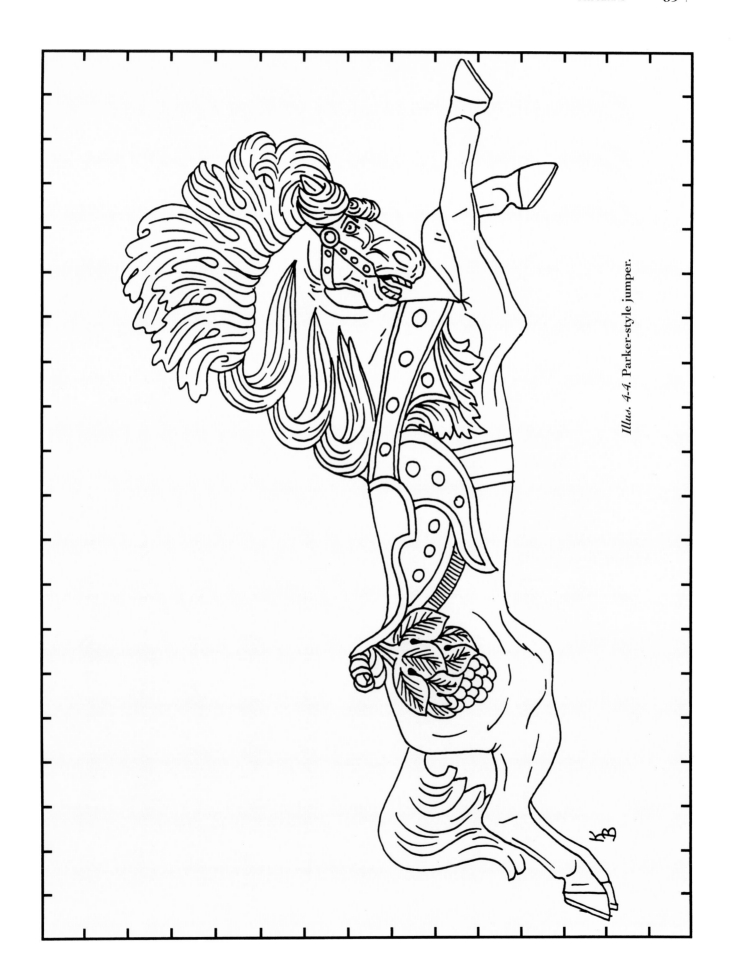

Illus. 4-4. Parker-style jumper.

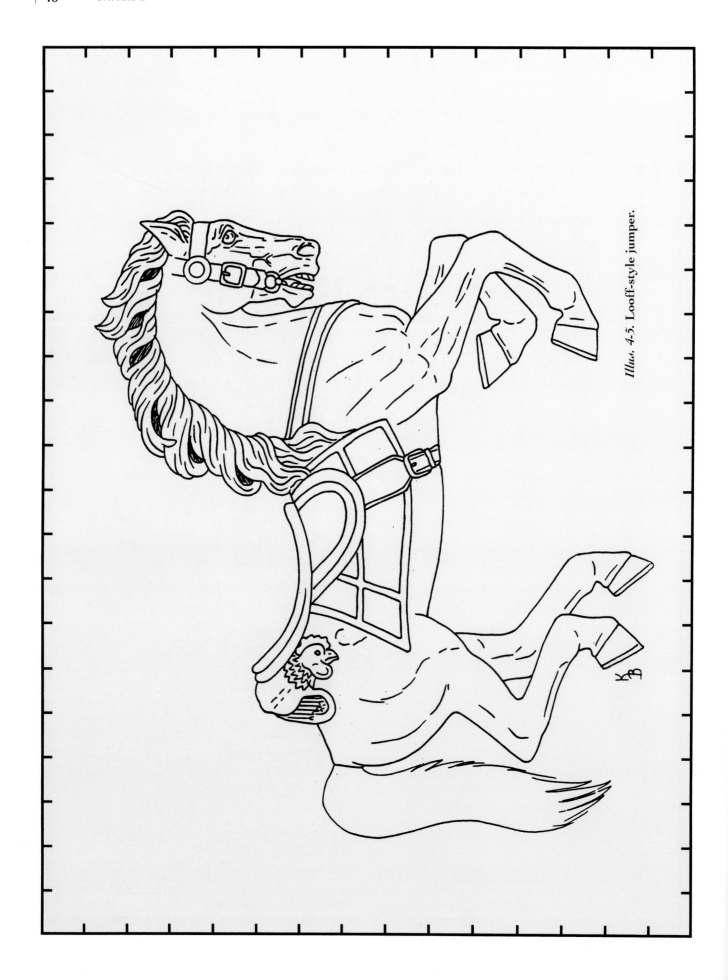

Illus. 4-5. Looff-style jumper.

Illus. 4-6. Herschell-style jumper.

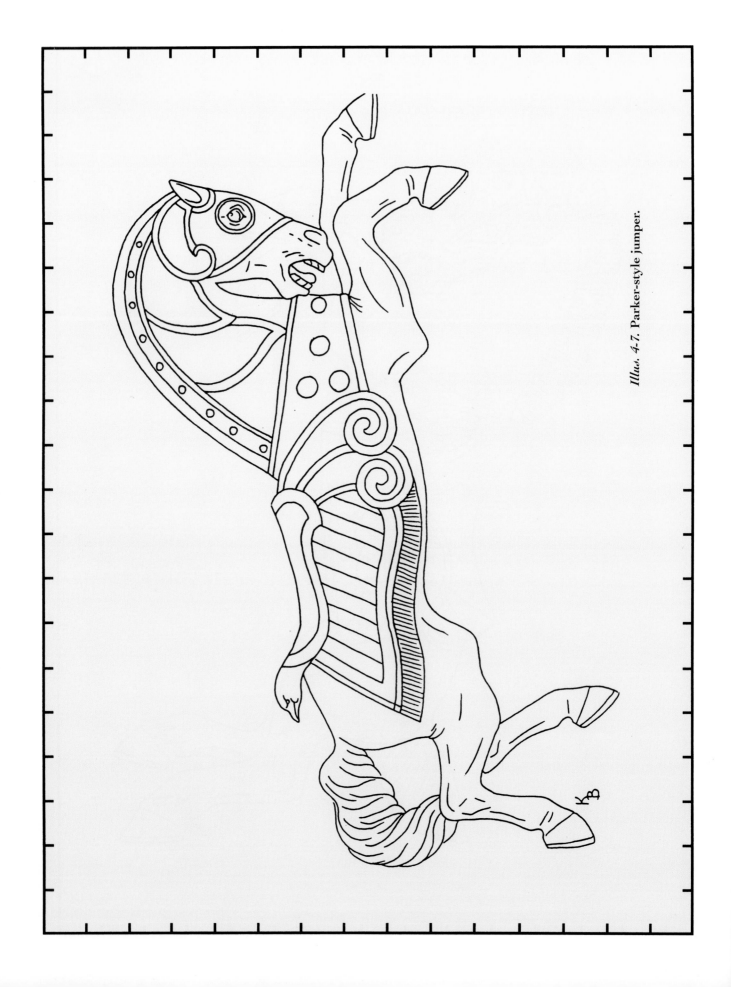

Illus. 4-7. Parker-style jumper.

Illus. 4-8. Illions-style jumper.

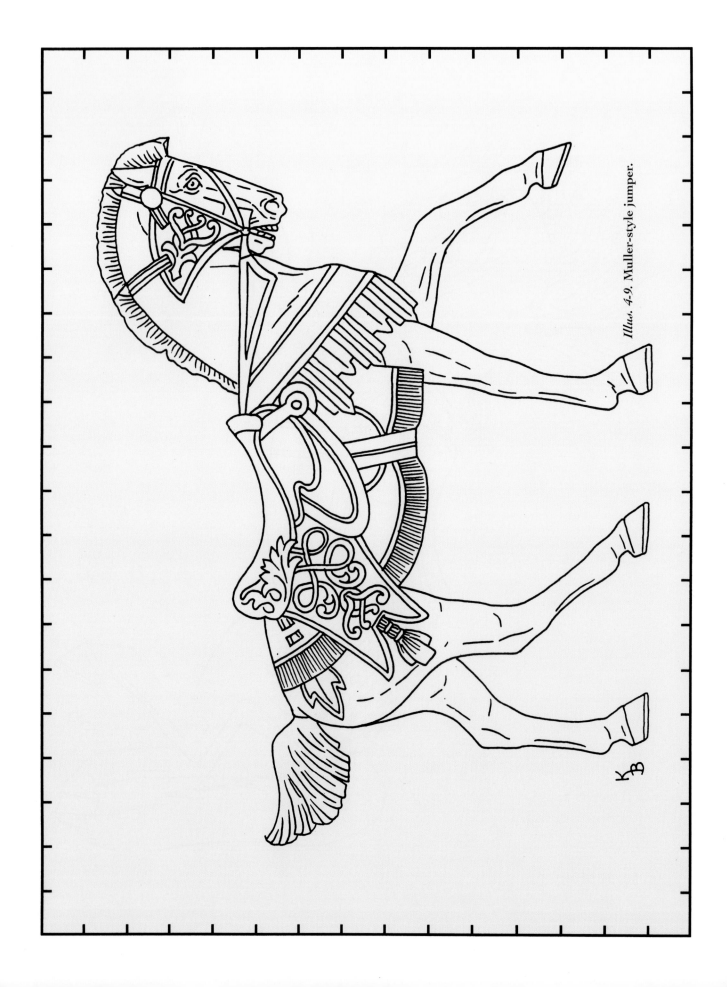

Illus. 4-9. Muller-style jumper.

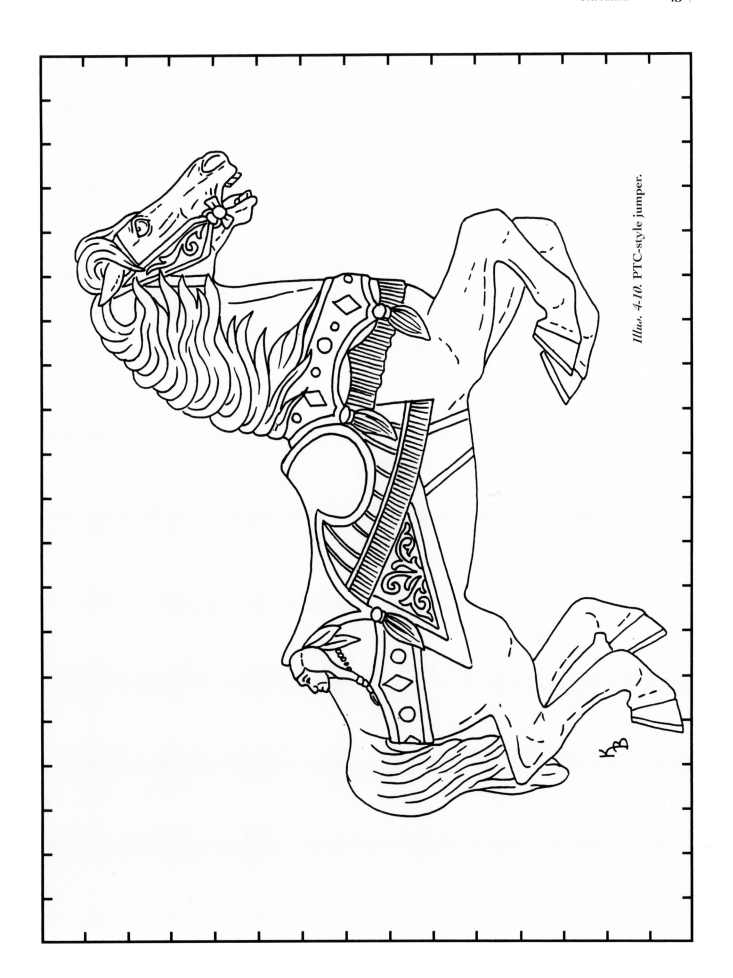

Illus. 4-10. PTC-style jumper.

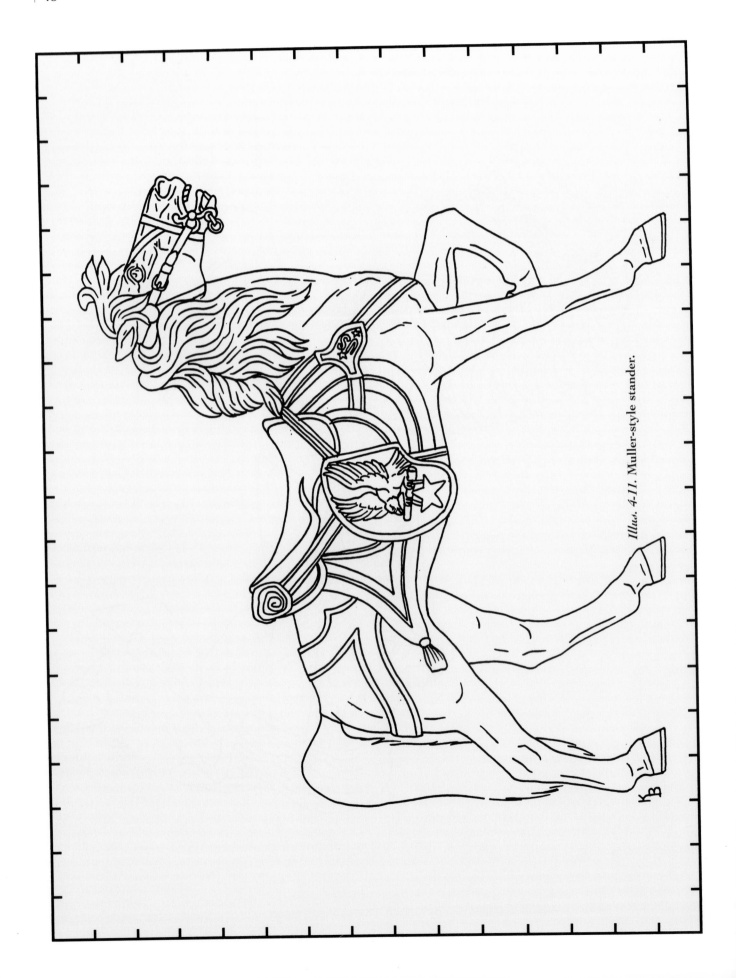

Illus. 4-11. Muller-style stander.

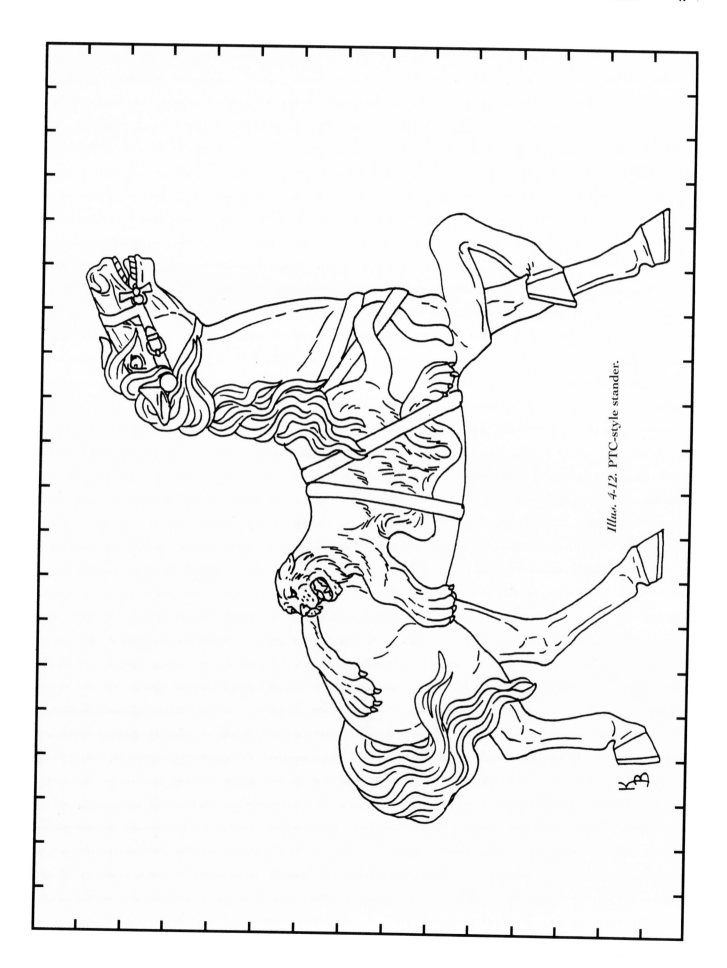

Illus. 4-12. PTC-style stander.

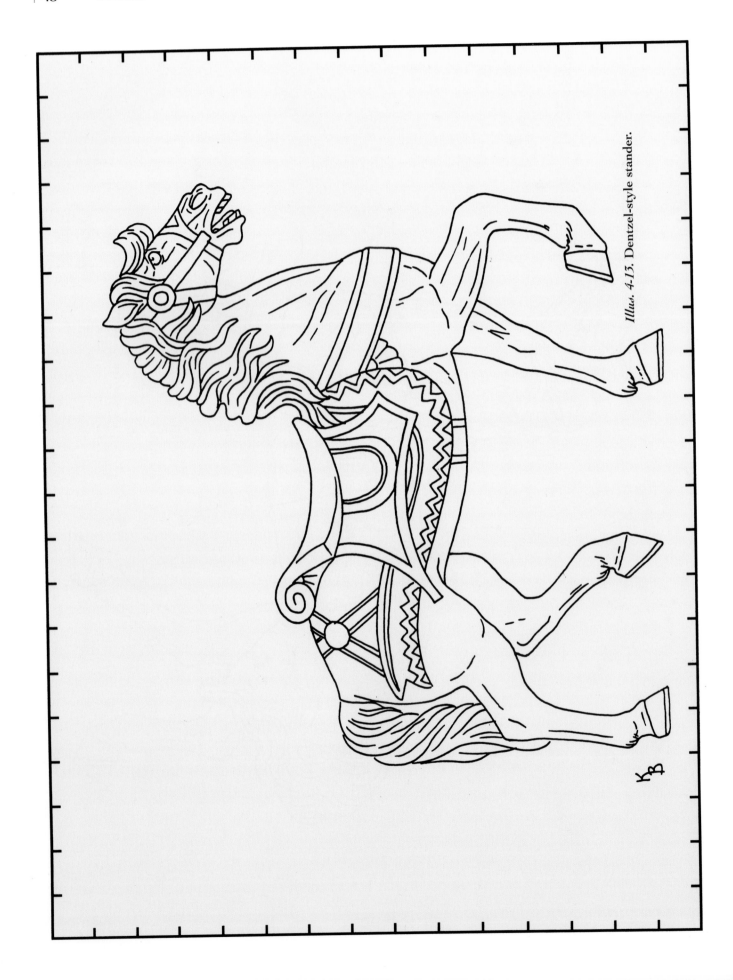

Illus. 4-13. Dentzel-style stander.

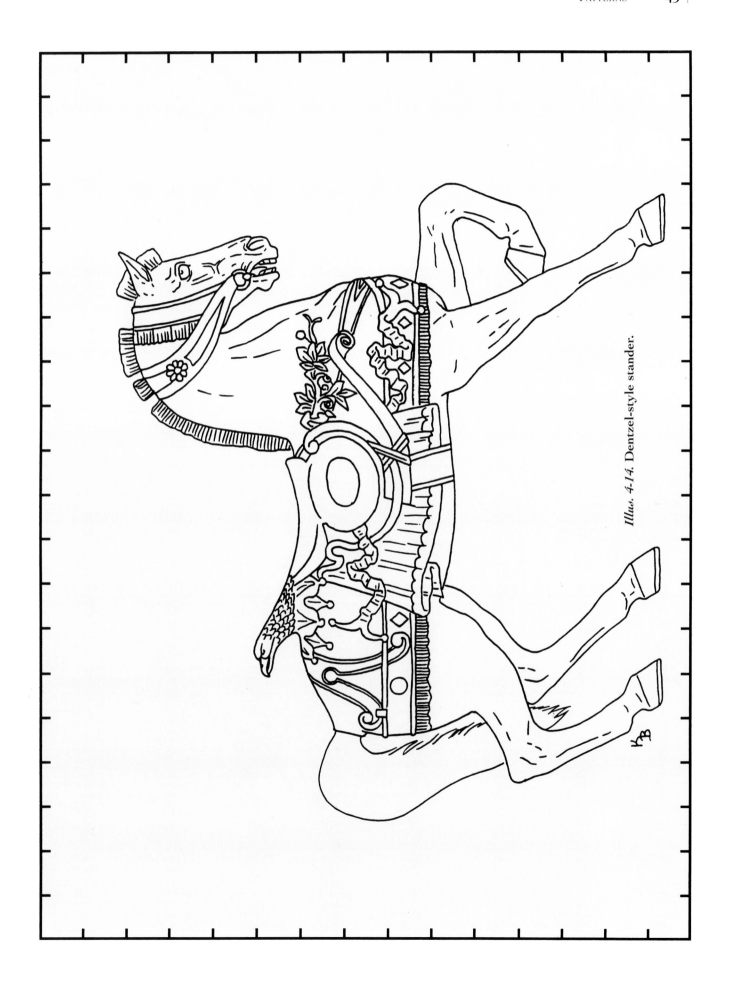

Illus. 4-14. Dentzel-style stander.

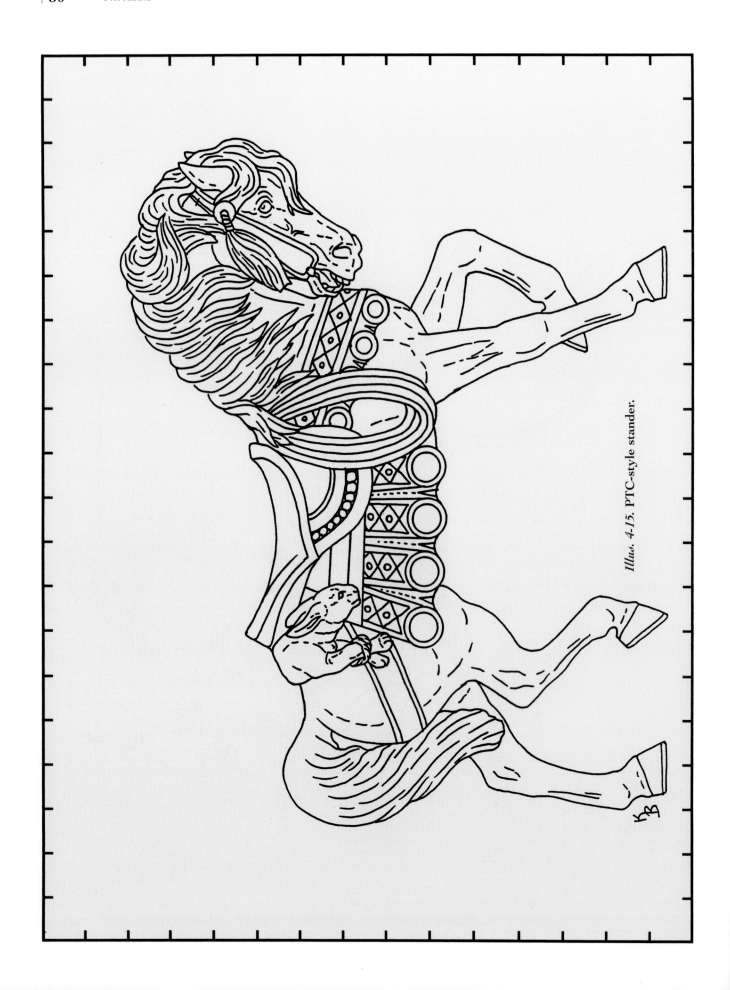

Illus. 4-15. PTC-style stander.

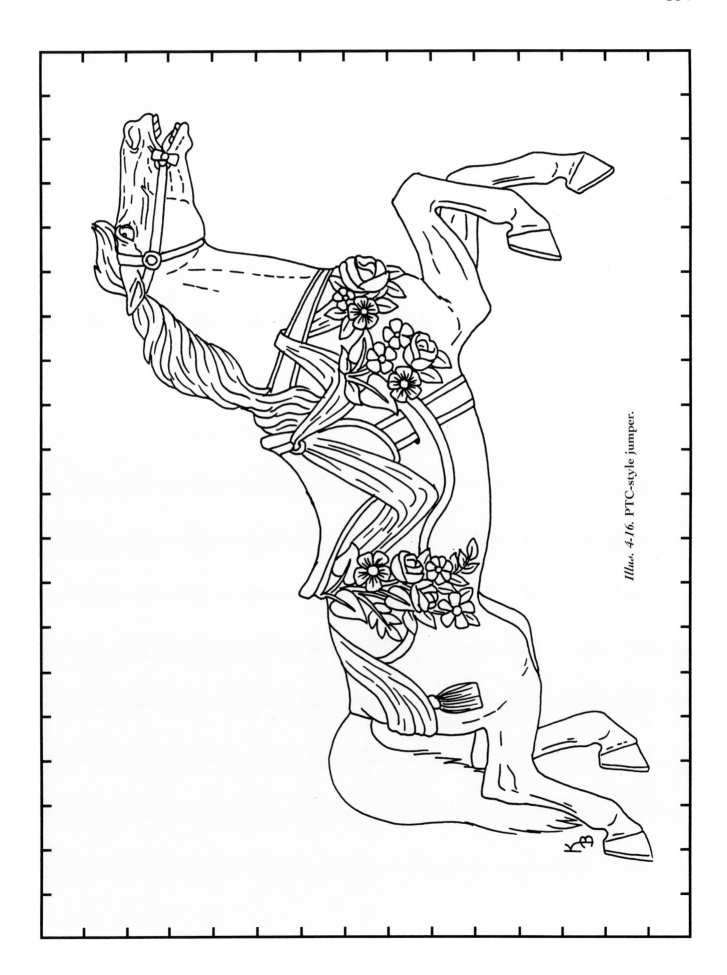

Illus. 4-16. PTC-style jumper.

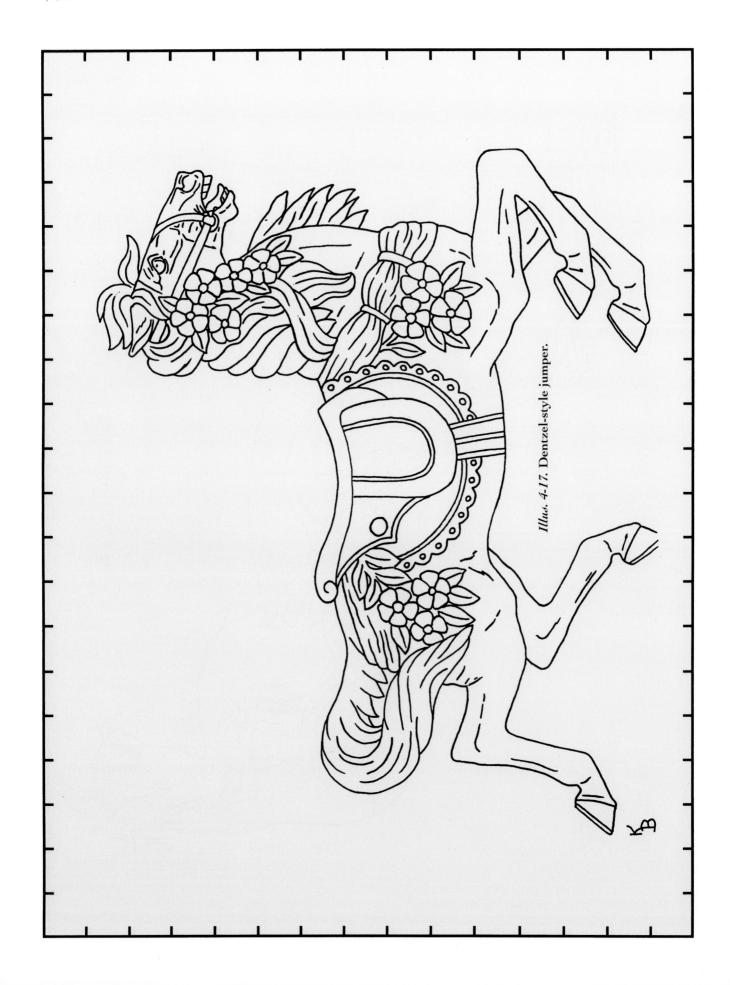

Illus. 4-17. Dentzel-style jumper.

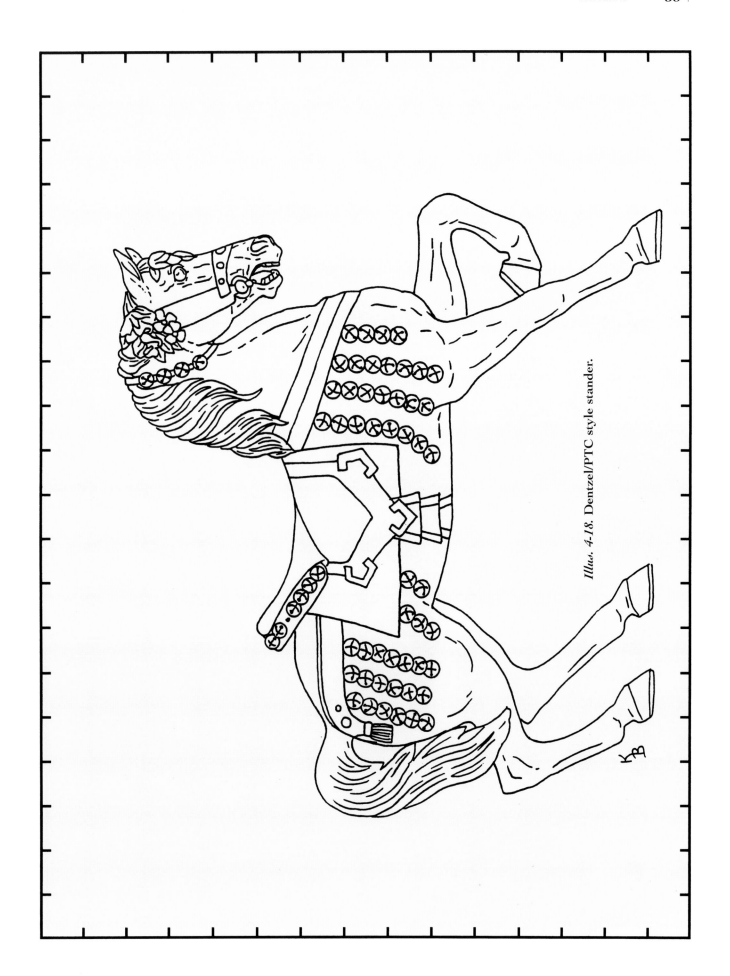

Illus. 4-18. Dentzel/PTC style stander.

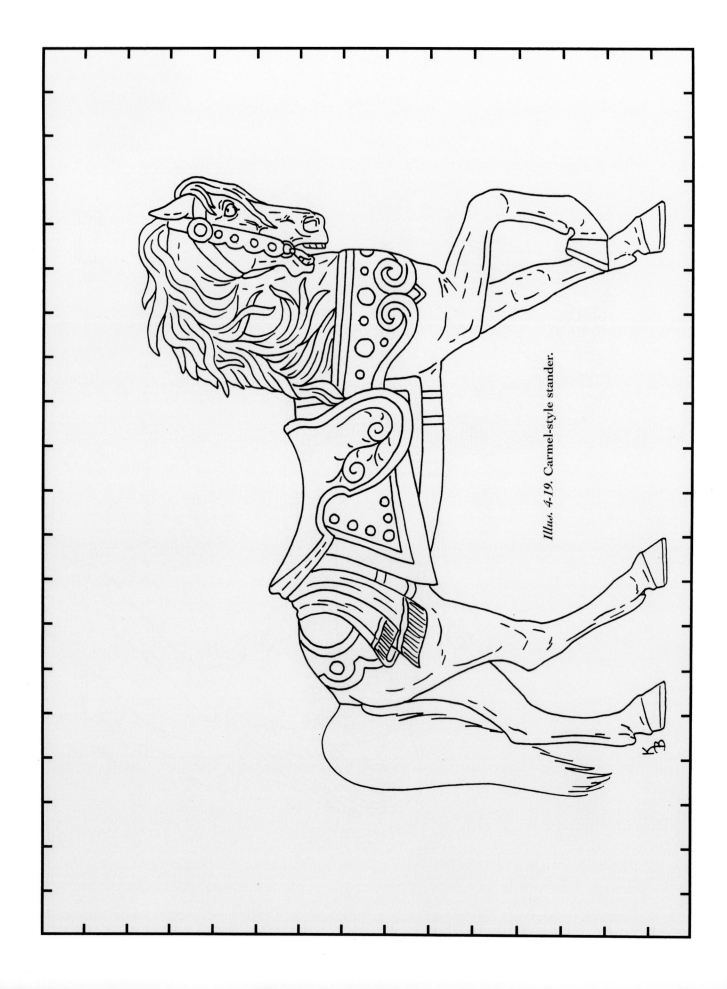

Illus. 4-19. Carmel-style stander.

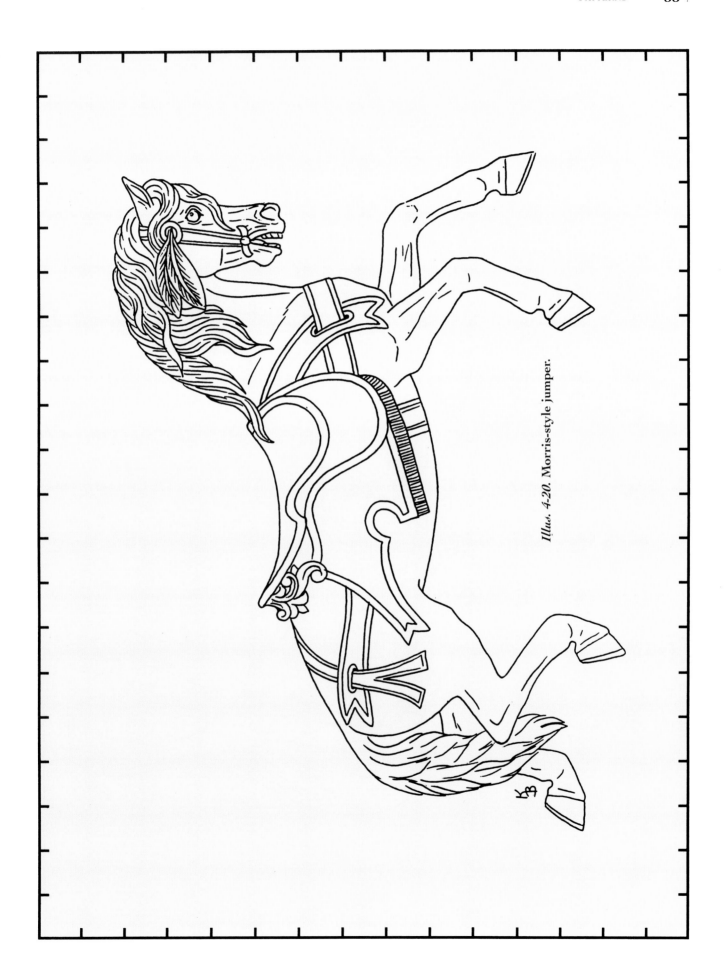

Illus. 4-20. Morris-style jumper.

Illus. 4-21. Illions-style stander.

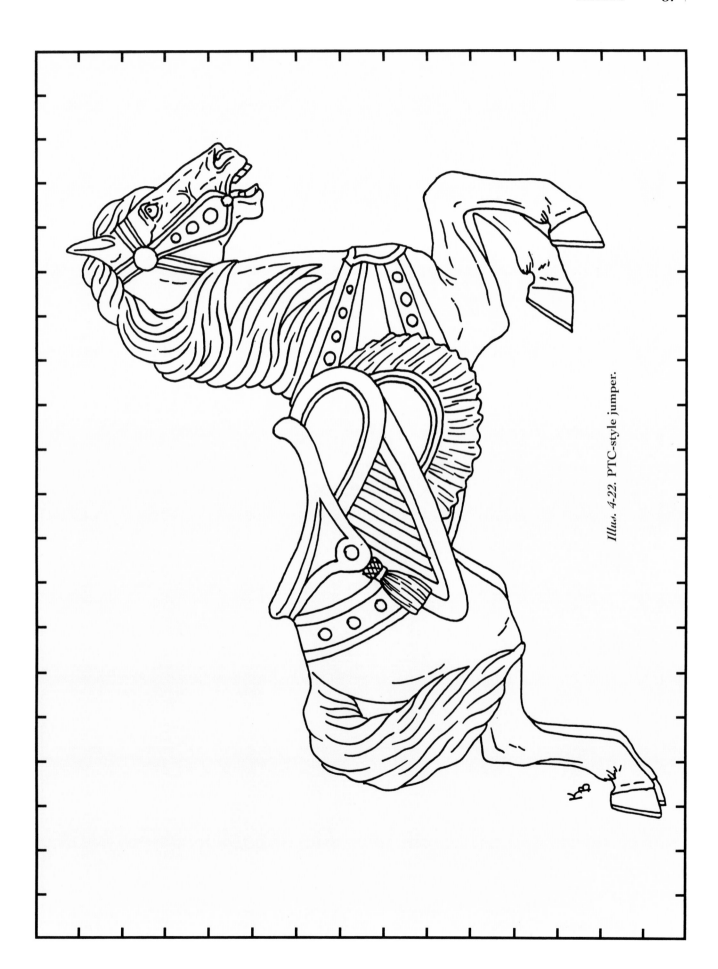

Illus. 4-22. PTC-style jumper.

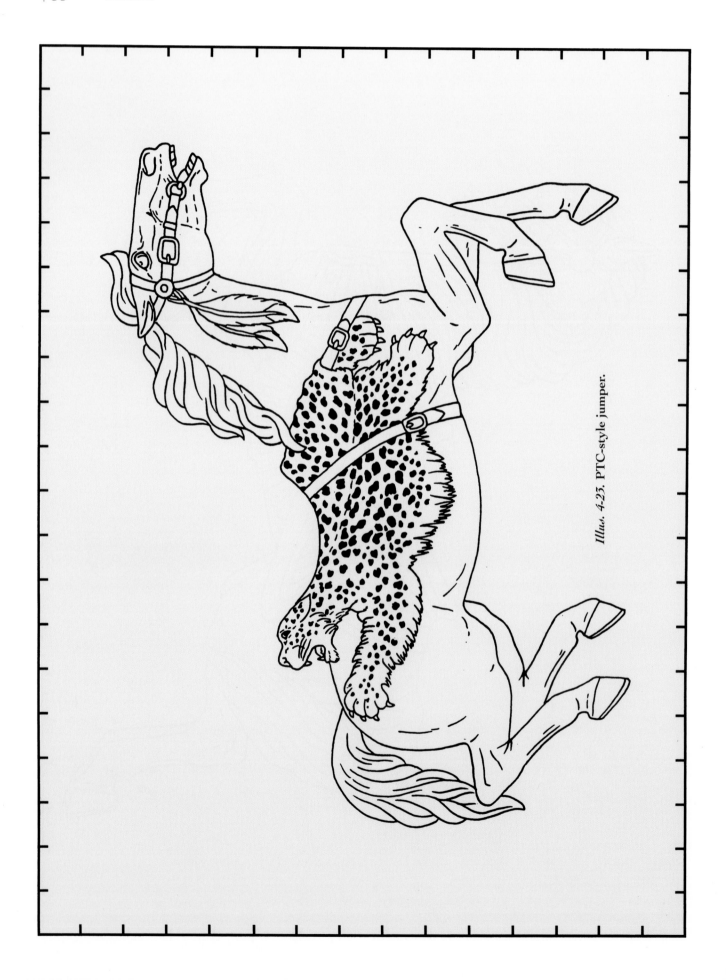

Illus. 4-23, PTC-style jumper.

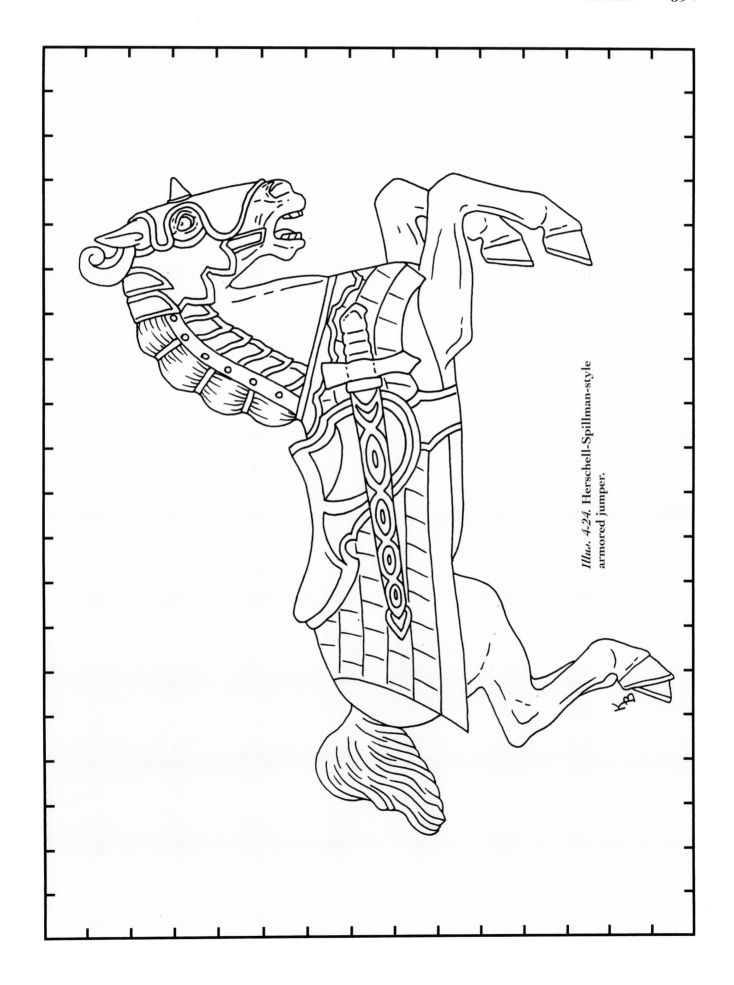

Illus. 4-24. Herschell-Spillman-style armored jumper.

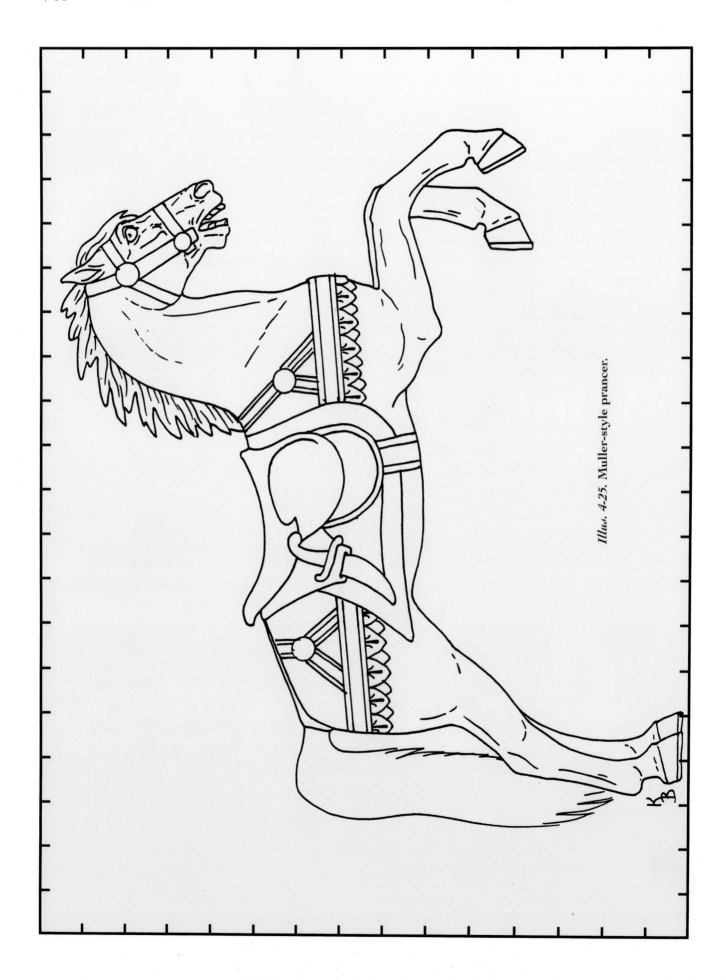

Illus. 4-25. Muller-style prancer.

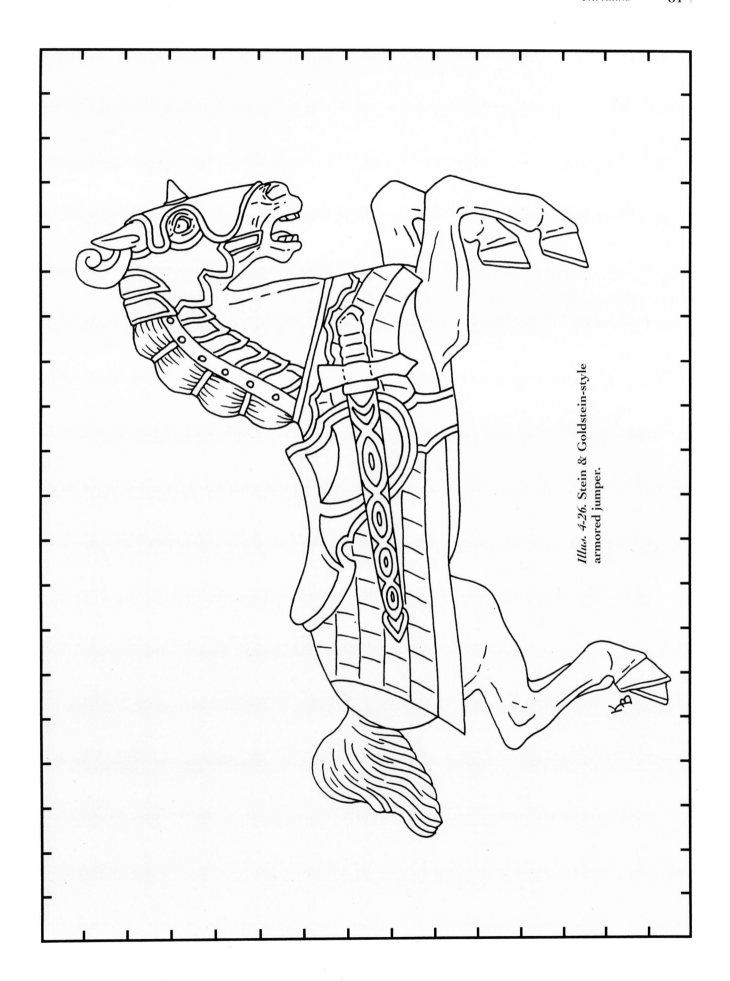

Illus. 4-26. Stein & Goldstein-style armored jumper.

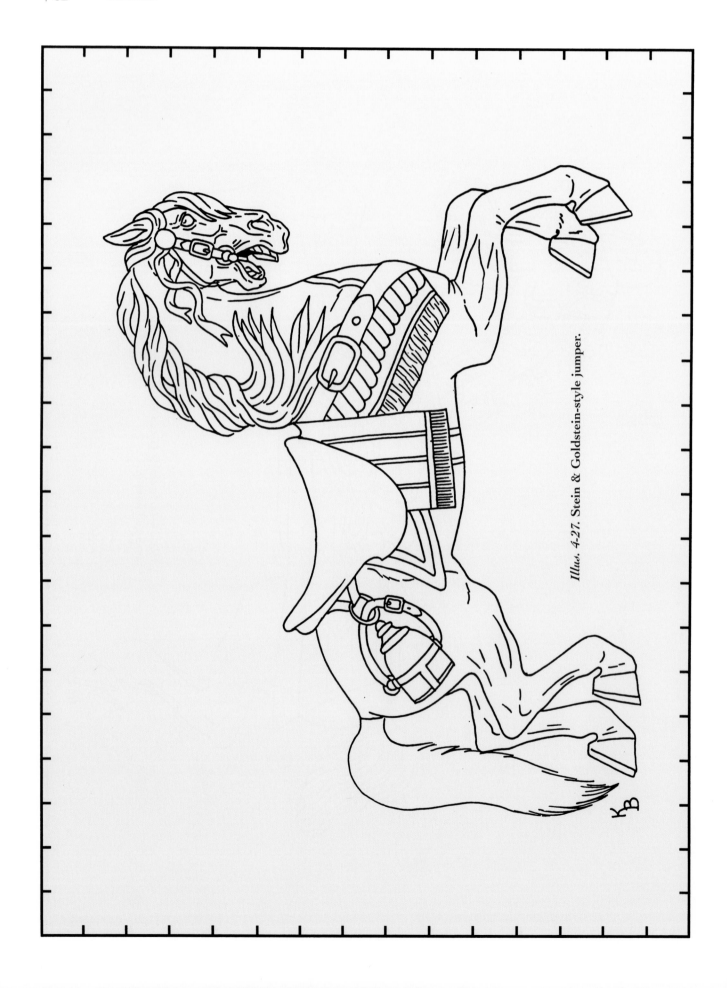

Illus. 4-27. Stein & Goldstein-style jumper.

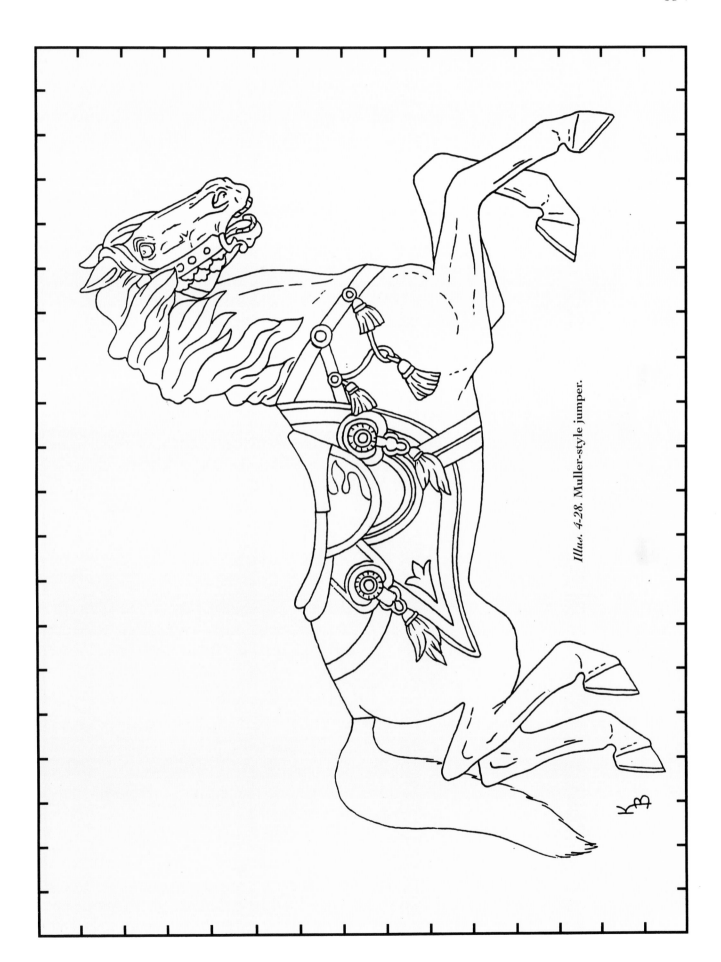

Illus. 4-28. Muller-style jumper.

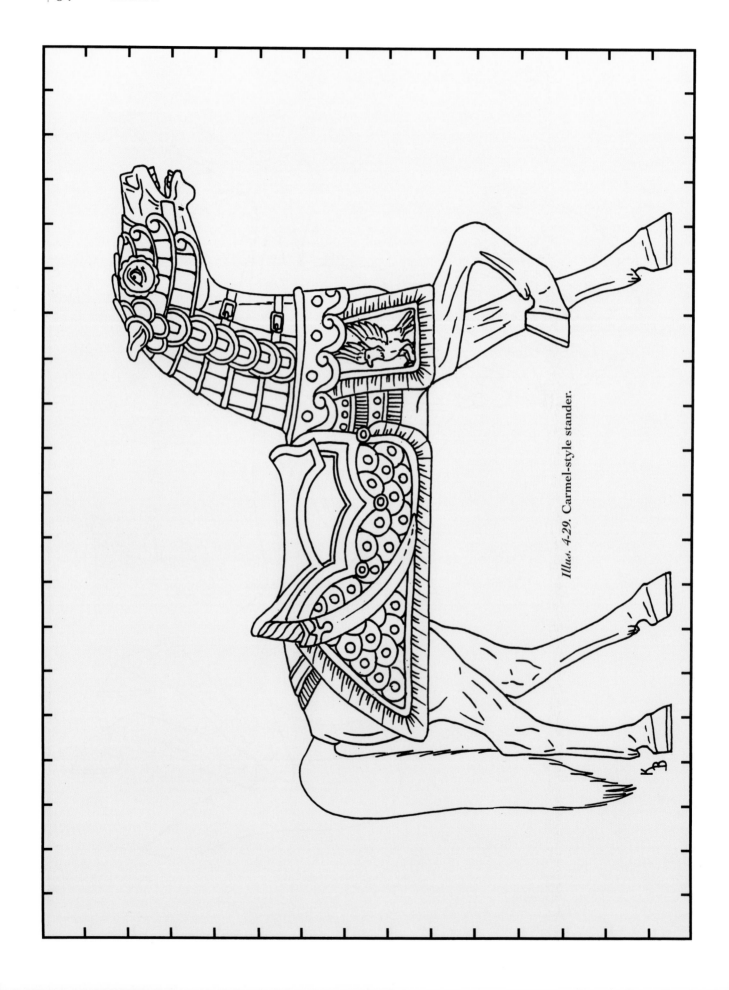

Illus. 4-29. Carmel-style stander.

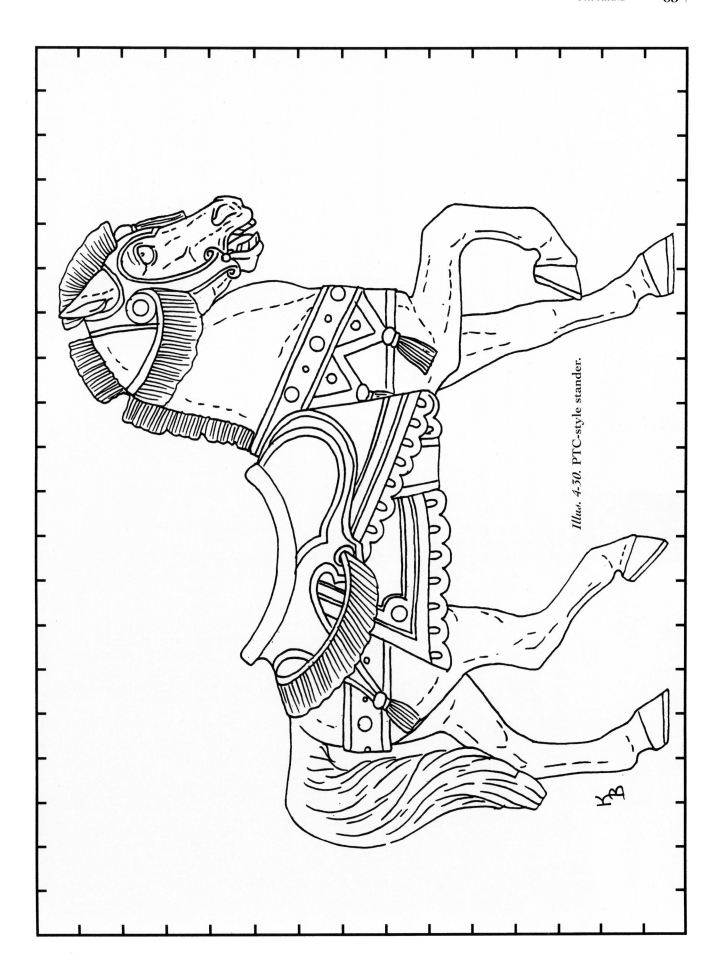

Illus. 4-30. PTC-style stander.

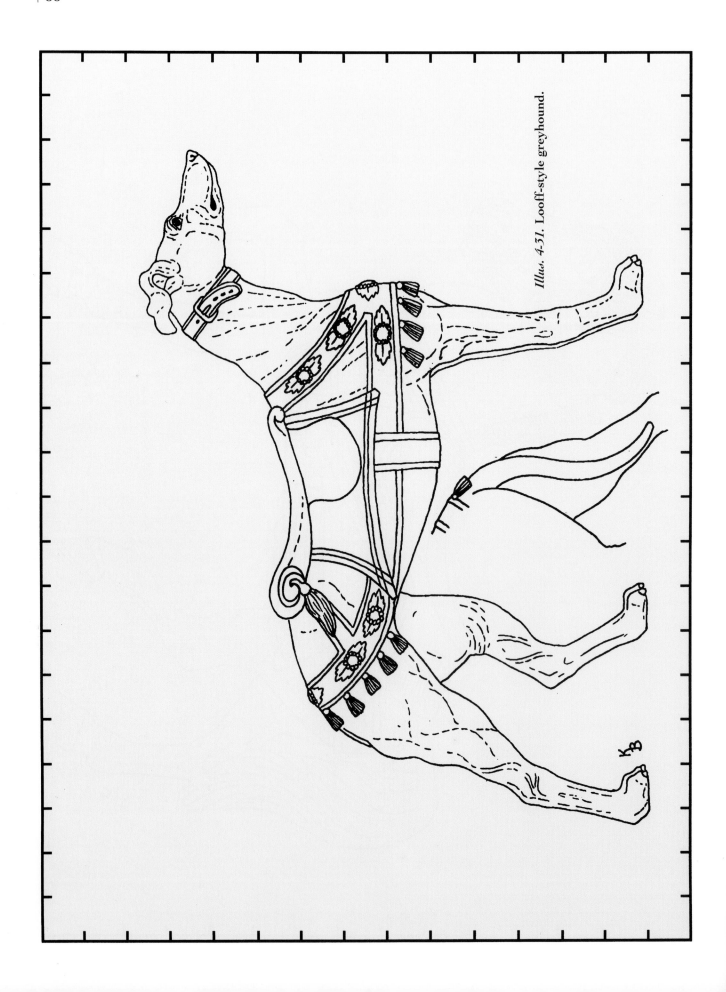

Illus. 4-31. Looff-style greyhound.

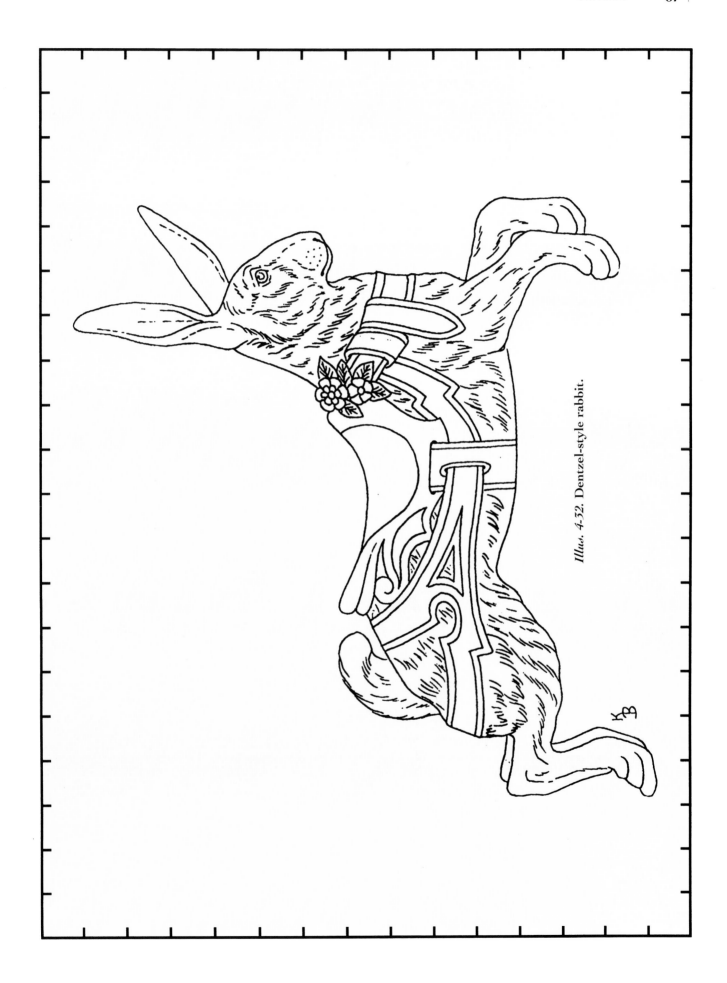

Illus. 4-32. Dentzel-style rabbit.

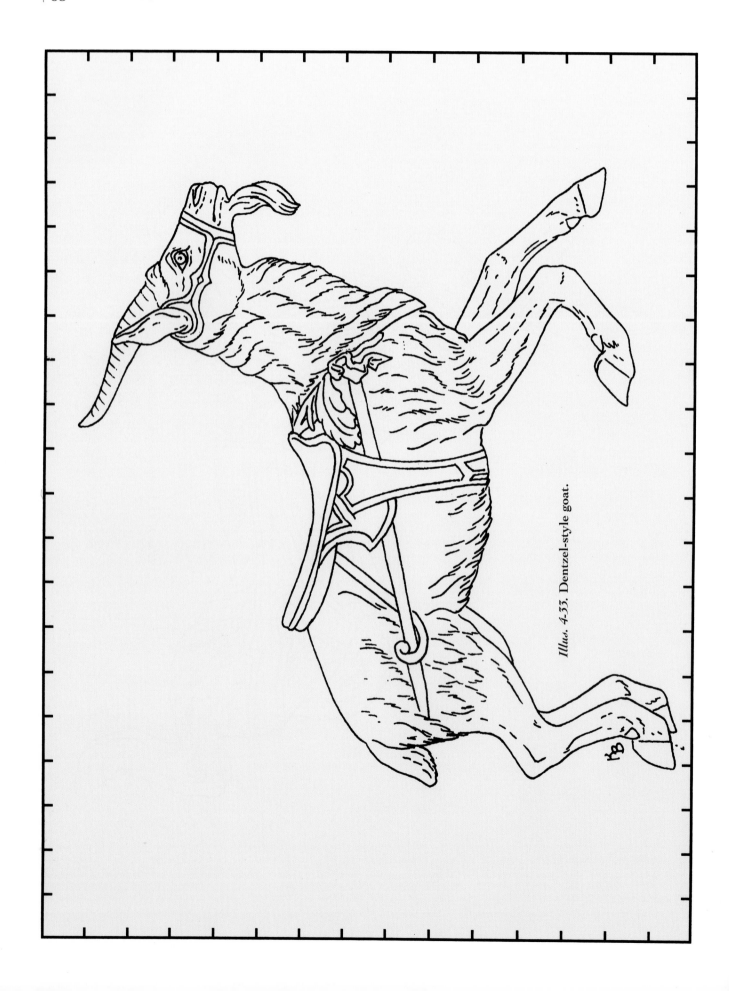

Illus. 4-33. Dentzel-style goat.

5

Carving Techniques

If you visit a wood-carving club, you'll likely find that many of the wood-carvers are self-taught. Most of our carvers at Horsin' Around have never held a chisel before coming to our school, and seem to have little problem. If you're an inexperienced carver, this chapter offers helpful tips on carving techniques, as well as solutions to problems that you will likely encounter when you start to carve your carousel animal. If you're reluctant to start carving on your own, you might consider taking a carving class that features large-figure carving, or picking up a carving book on carving-in-the-round. You need to have confidence when handling carving tools, so spending a little time developing that confidence is worth the effort.

BASIC CARVING TECHNIQUE FOR BEGINNERS

As discussed earlier, if you need to remove a large amount of wood—such as when you rough out your animal blank to get closer to your finished size—using a mallet to drive a large chisel or gouge is a good idea. To do this, grip the tool handle in your left hand (if you are right-handed), as shown in Illus. 5-1. Then position the blade end at an angle on the wood in the area you need to work, and tap the end of the wood handle with the mallet. If you've never done this before, try it on a piece of scrap wood. Also, avoid using a large mallet with a small-bladed tool; you might break your tool. (Note: Always clamp your wood down before working on it. Don't ever try to steady a loose piece of wood with a hand or other part of your body.)

When you need more control (such as when carving detail), you can guide the tool using both hands. To do this, grip the shaft of the tool below the handle with your left hand (if you are right-handed), and grip the handle with your right hand. Position the blade end at an angle on the wood in the area you need to work, and then push with your right hand while you guide the tool with your left hand. Once again, you can try this on a clamped-down piece of wood until you feel comfortable.

Illus. 5-1. **Using a large gouge and mallet to carve a horse head.**

When carving a carousel animal, knowing how to use a V-parting tool is crucial. The V-parting tool is used to outline the lines of almost any detail you carve on the animal. We recommend you use a mallet to carefully drive your V-parting tool, because it will give you more control when outlining. (You won't believe this until you try it, so go ahead and try it both with a mallet and without one.)

To learn to use a V-parting tool, clamp a piece of wood to a table, and then draw a straight line on the carving surface of the wood. Grip the handle of the V-parting tool with your left hand (if you are right-handed), and hold the mallet in your right hand. Position the point of the V-parting tool on the beginning of the line. Then rotate the tool so that the right side of the V is straight up and down.

Now, gently tap the mallet to move the V-parting tool, being careful to keep the tool positioned on the line. Continue tapping gently until you have gone the length of the line. If you've done it correctly, you will have carved a groove along the line, but the right side of the groove will be a straight up-and-down cut. If you were outlining a feature, the wood on the right side would be left

69

high (to protrude), and the wood on the left side would be your waste.

As mentioned before, you use the V-parting tool to outline the details before you carve them. For example, when you draw a strap on the side of your horse's head, you would use the V-parting tool to outline the lines (edges) of the strap. Since the strap will protrude from the horse's head, after carving your line you would start carving away the part that wasn't the strap (it will be cut deeper on that side anyway because you rotated the V-parting tool), leaving the strap alone to be the more prominent element.

WORKING WITH WOOD GRAIN

As you start carving, you will quickly get a feel for how the wood responds. If you carve in one direction, the chisel will seem to just glide through the wood, but when you reverse direction, it will fight you all the way by producing checks and cracks in the wood. Listen to the wood. If it starts to crack or chip, change direction. You will start to do this without thinking about it as you become more experienced.

As you carve, try to carve cross grain when in a tight place. If you build your animal by following our directions, there will be very little end grain to deal with. If you have to cut into end grain, do it with care or it will split and break off in large pieces. By the way, you can use this to your advantage if you need to remove large amounts of wood.

CARVING AN ANIMAL USING A BLUEPRINT

For most beginners, visualizing the three-dimensional object (your animal) from the two-dimensional drawing (your blueprint) is a difficult task. One of the best ways to solve this problem is to surround yourself with small, realistic plastic models of horses or whatever animal you are carving, and as many drawings and photographs as you can get your hands on—showing the animal at different kinds of angles. Good, accurate animal models and toys can be expensive, so check your local flea market first.

Study your models and look at your roughed-out blank, and try to see how they correspond. Concentrate on which features protrude, which are recessed, what surface is high, what surface is low, where the angles are, what part of the animal slopes and what doesn't, etc. With practice, you will start to see the animal in the wood.

CARVING FROM SQUARE TO ROUND

Animals are rounded, not square. This is obvious, but rounding a carving to make curves instead of carving large flat areas is a difficult problem for beginners. One point to remember is that you round from the center of an area, not from the edges. (Rounding from the edges will give you a flat area with rounded edges, not a curve.) As shown in Illus. 5-2, determine where the highest point of the curve will be, and start rounding from there.

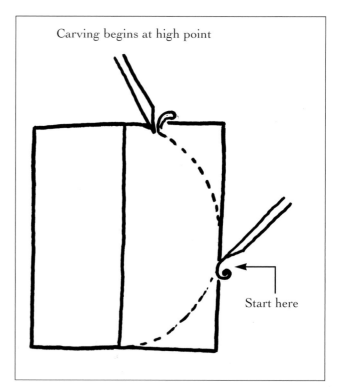

Illus. 5-2. **Round from the center of the area, not from the edges.**

USING THE PROPER TOOL FOR THE JOB

Using the right tool will save you both time and effort. Beginners tend to get used to a particular-size gouge and use it for everything. This isn't fatal, but if the blade is small and you're carving in an area where you need to remove large amounts of wood, it's going to take you forever, whereas a larger gouge will save you time. By the same token, using too large a gouge can force you to be extremely cautious in small areas, which also wastes your time. Stop every so often and reevaluate the tool you are using.

FIXING MISTAKES

One of the first things we tell new students at Horsin' Around is that almost every mistake you can make while carving your animal can be fixed, either with some carveable wood putty (available in woodworking stores and catalogs) or with a replacement piece of wood. Use putty when the mistake is small and the area has no danger of breaking off. For larger areas and areas that have to bear some pressure, cut out the offending wood and glue in a replacement chunk. If you paint your animal, no one will ever see the mistake. (Note: If you plan to apply an oil or stain to your animal rather than paint it, you will want to avoid using putty because it will show.)

Illus. 5-3.

6

Animal Anatomy

You can't carve an animal if you don't know what it looks like. This would seem obvious, but of all the problems carousel carvers have carving their animals, animal anatomy stands out as most common. Most beginners try to draw and carve their animals with little research on their anatomy or even the animals' general look. Since carving a large animal is really a type of sculpting, you need to be familiar with the animal's shape and curves.

How realistic does your carving have to look? That's really up to you. Most antique carousel animals were carved for function and to last a long time. Things such as height and length were decided based on how easy it was for youngsters to climb on and off the animal. The animals were often thinner than the real animals so little legs could straddle the bodies, and certain areas were reinforced and made thicker so they could take abuse without breaking off. In other words, realistic-looking animal anatomy was sacrificed somewhat for function.

An exception are the carvings of Daniel Muller, who grew up in Gustav Dentzel's carving shop. Daniel spent many hours at night in sculpture classes, and carved his beautiful horses and other animals in a very realistic style, which is prized by collectors. John Zalar, who worked for the Philadelphia Toboggan Co. and later for Charles

Looff, was another carver who preferred realism in his carousel carvings.

The point of this discussion is that most carousel animals were not meant to look exactly like real animals, and if you have chosen a style of animal that is not particularly realistic, familiarize yourself with the real animal's basic characteristics, but don't drive yourself crazy trying to carve every muscle precisely. If you've chosen to emulate the style of Muller or Zalar, however, you'll want to pay closer attention to anatomy. But again, remember you're carving a wooden animal, not cloning a real animal.

That said, we still can't stress enough how useful a good book on animal anatomy can be while you're carving. Check with your local library and bookstore to find one. Another way to learn about animal anatomy is to get a good plastic model or realistic toy version of your animal and study it. Look at it from all different angles, and see where the bones and muscles are prominent. It's helpful if you can find a model in a stance similar to your animal's if you prefer the realistic styles of carousel animals, since different features are prominent in different stances.

To get you started, refer to Illus. 6-1. It displays the basic anatomy of a horse, with its different parts labeled.

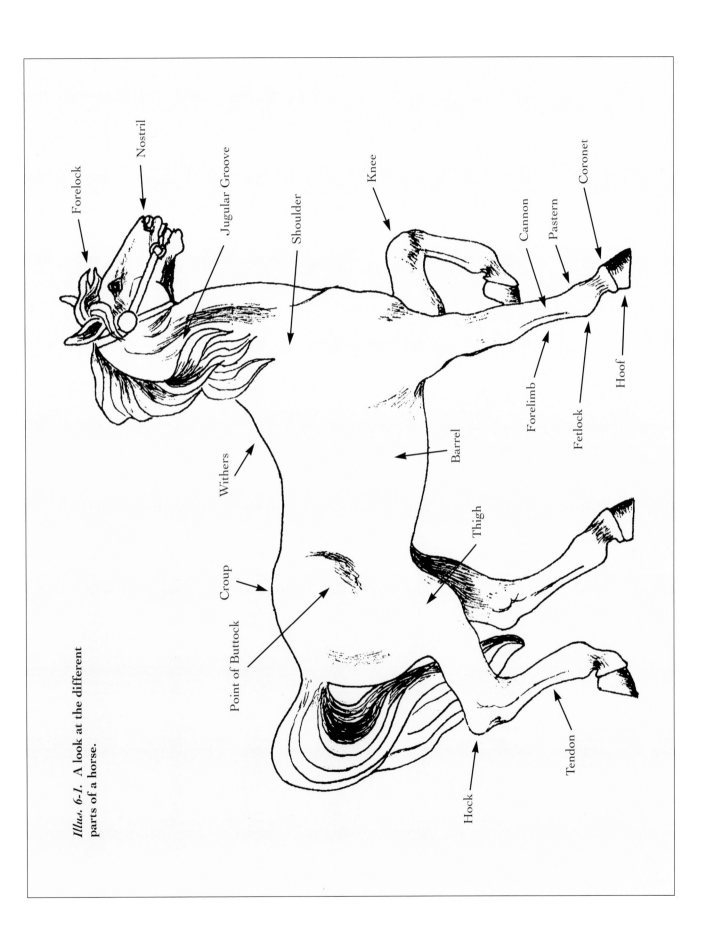

Illus. 6-1. A look at the different parts of a horse.

PART TWO

Building and Carving Your Carousel Animal

Y ou've picked which animal to carve, gathered some tools, bought your wood, and made your blueprint. Now, it's the moment of truth. You're going to have to actually start cutting, gluing, and carving your animal.

If you're not an experienced carver, you're likely experiencing some doubt about now and starting to think up excuses for quitting before you start. Before you get too panicked, though, remember that while carving a wooden carousel animal is a type of artistic expression, it's not some mysterious process. It involves specific techniques and skills that can be taught and learned. If you're feeling

particularly nervous, consider these points:

1. You're not going to carve your animal all at once. You're going to carve it one small step at a time. Focus on the step you're on, and forget about the next one until you get there.

2. It doesn't matter how long it takes you to carve your animal as long as you enjoy each moment you're working on it.

3. There are very few mistakes you can make that are so bad they can't be fixed.

4. If you get totally stumped, you can always find a friendly wood-carver or two in your community to help you out. After all, you're now part of the wood-carving family in their eyes! And they love to give advice!

7

Precarving Advice

Since this book doesn't focus on carving one particular animal, we can't give you step-by-step carving directions. Instead, we guide you with directions that can be applied to whatever animal you've chosen to carve. These directions include such things as what is the best part of the animal to carve first, how to approach carving each piece, anatomical features to be aware of, and particular mistakes to avoid.

Most of the instructions pertain to carousel horses, since they are by far the most common carousel animal, but information is added where useful for people carving menagerie animals. If youre carving a menagerie animal and you are confused about how something should look, consult your photographs or pattern, a good plastic model or realistic toy, and a good animal-anatomy book for guidance.

In addition to the instructions, each chapter features a special section called the Carving Gallery. In carving carousel animals, a picture really is worth a thousand words. The Carving Galleries contain close-up photographs of different carved animal features—eyes, ears, knees, etc.—so you will know what they are supposed to look like. If you know what a feature looks like, you can carve it, so refer to these photographs often as you carve.

Each chapter also features a Common Mistakes section, which will point out some of the common errors we've seen beginning carousel carvers make. The best way to use this section is to read it after you've read about carving a particular part, but before you actually start to carve it.

ANIMAL DIMENSIONS

One of the greatest concerns you'll have when you start carving is how big the animals parts should be. The following tables provide some useful guidelines on the average dimensions of the different parts of carousel horses and some of the common menagerie animals. Table 7-1 provides dimension guidelines based on the outside-row (large), middle-row (medium), and inner-row (small jumper) Philadelphia-style horses. Table 7-2 provides dimension guidelines for an armored horse (since the armor increases the size of certain features of the horse), and some of the more popular menagerie animals.

Be aware these numbers are just guidelines, and may not pertain exactly to your animal. For example, if you've chosen to carve a replica of a very muscular military horse, your horse may need to be bulkier in its legs and breast than the average carousel horse. Ultimately, you should rely on your own best judgment and your eyes for proportion. When your animal is finished, people are not going to measure the different parts of it to see if its accurate; they are just going to look at it.

If you look at your animal and think one area is too fat (even though it matches the dimensions in the table), make it smaller until it looks to be in correct proportion to the rest of your animal. The beauty of your animal is going to depend on how the dimensions of every part are proportioned in relation to the other parts, not to some measurements in a table.

SOME IMPORTANT INSTRUCTIONS BEFORE YOU START

Each chapter in Part 2 addresses a single section of the animal. For each section, you will start by cutting out and gluing up your pieces, progress to pegging with wooden dowels (when necessary), and then do the carving.

Before you begin, there are a few things you need to know:

1. Cut out all your pieces with the band saw before you glue them up to make blanks. Sawing pieces out of boards that have already been laminated is more difficult and could cause you to break the band-saw blade.

2. When you are carving, keep the photograph or pattern of the animal you are carving on your worktable at all times, and refer to it over and over again while shaping your animal. Since paper can take a beating around tools, we often slip our pho-

Guideline Dimensions for Average Philadelphia-Style Horses
(in inches)

DIMENSION	SMALL	MEDIUM	LARGE
Length of breast to rump	31	34½	46
Width of head (including average mane)	4¾	5½	7
Width of nose	2¾	3	4
Width of neck at body joint	6¾–7⅖	7½–8¼	10–11
Width of body at pole	7⅖	8¼	11
Width of saddle back	5⅖	6	8
Width of rump	8	9	12
Width of front legs at body joint	2¾	3	4
Width of legs at knee	2–2½	2¼–2$\frac{13}{16}$	3–3¾
Width of hind legs at body joint	4	4½	6
Length of hoof	3–3⅖	3⅛–3¾	4½–5
Width of hoof	2⅕–2¾	2$\frac{7}{16}$–3	3¼–4
Width of widest point of tail	4	4½	6

Table 7-1. **Dimensions for Philadelphia-style horses.**

Guideline Dimensions for Armored Horse and Menagerie Animals
(in inches)

DIMENSION	ARMORED HORSE	TIGER	LION	RABBIT	GIRAFFE	GOAT	CAT
Length of breast to rump	48	47	55	37	37	37	37½
Width of head	9	10	20 (with mane)	10	8	8	8¾*
Width of nose	3½	5½	6	4	4	3	1
Width of neck at body joint	16	10	14	8	7	10½	7½
Width of body at pole	18	13½	14	11	12	12	8½
Width of saddle back	17	13½	11½	11	11½	9½	8
Width of rump	18	11	14	11	11	12	8
Width of front legs at body joint	4	5	6	4	5	4	3
Width of legs at knee	3	4½	3½ (front/4 rear)	3	4	3½	2
Width of hind legs at body joint	9	5½	7	5½	5½	6	4
Length of hoof/paw	4½	7	8	4	4½	4	5
Width of hoof/paw	3½	5	7	3½	3¼	3½	4

*Including something in mouth, such as fish or small animal

Table 7-2. **Dimensions for an armored horse and menagerie animals.**

tographs and patterns inside a clear plastic sleeve (such as the sheet protectors that fit in three-ring binders) to keep them from getting torn or bent.

If using an illustration in a book, you might want to tear it out of the book (some people buy a used or second copy of the book to cut up) or have it scanned into a computer and printed out on a color printer. One advantage of having a photograph scanned into a computer is that you can then enlarge the photograph by sections to get a better look at detail. If you don't have ready access to a scanner, check with your full-service copy centers or call a local photography supply store to find who does that kind of work in your community.

3. Always clamp your piece to a worktable or in a vise before trying to carve it. Don't ever try to steady a piece of wood with your arm or your body while you try to carve it. First, its really dangerous to use a sharp chisel on an unstable chunk of wood. Second, it will result in a bad mistake when the piece shifts. When clamping, if the clamp starts to dent the wood, insert a piece of scrap wood between the clamp and the piece youre carving.

4. As you're carving, carve both sides of an anatomical area at the same time. For example, don't finish carving one side of the muzzle (nose and mouth area) before you start carving the other side of the muzzle. Carve a little on one side of the nose, and then carve a similar amount on the other side so that the two sides stay in rough proportion the whole time. By the same token, after you have carved some of the muzzle area, move back to the cheekbone areas and do some carving there to keep the head roughly in proportion at all times. Once you have all the features of a piece shaped, you will then reduce wood all over the piece, bit by bit, to reach your finished size.

5. After you have glued up the blanks of the head and body, you will have to draw a centerline over the top of the pieces. Dont ever carve on or across that line unless absolutely necessary, such as when lowering wood so a strap crossing the centerline can be in relief.

The centerline should basically still be intact when you are completely finished carving your horse. Why? Since you made your blueprint from a side view of a finished carousel animal (or scale drawing of one), the silhouette of your horse is the one dimension that is correct without any alteration (carving). You will use that centerline to keep your horse in proportion. For example, after you have carved some on the nose, if you get in front of the nose and look down the centerline, you'll be able to tell if one half of the nose is fatter than the other half by measuring (or eyeing) how far one half extends out from the centerline in comparison to the other half. Draw your centerline and then use it.

6. Many carvers find it useful to mark with an X areas of wood that must be removed, so they don't get confused. Remember that all the markings you put on your animal can be carved or sanded off later, so write on the wood when it helps you keep things straight.

7. After you've carved a section to your satisfaction, go ahead and sand it. Review Chapter 13, Sanding Your Animal, for tips on how to do this.

8. As we mentioned in Part 1, if you don't work regularly in three dimensions, do yourself a favor and surround yourself with plastic models of your animal, books or photos showing your kind of animal from different angles, and a good animal-anatomy book.

9. And now, the single most important thing to remember when you are carving: Use a sharp blade!

8

Preparing and Carving the Head and Neck

No matter how fancy or dramatic the trappings, when a person looks at a well-carved carousel animal the first thing he really focuses on is the head. That's because the head and face are what give the animal its personality. The look of the eyes, the toss of the mane, the position of the ears—all these things give the animal a certain attitude. If you're carving a replica of an antique, keep the original animal's personality in mind as you carve.

MAKING CARVING BLANKS FOR THE HEAD AND NECK

When you made your blueprint in Chapter 3, you should have made an extra blueprint copy of the head and neck. Cut out the extra pattern for your animal's head and neck, and divide it at the cutting line where the head meets the neck. Then trace the two pattern pieces onto the wood. If a pattern piece is too big to fit on one plank, line up two planks and trace the pattern across the two.

For a Horse:

As shown in Illus. 8-1, a large head will require three layers of 2-inch-thick boards, with a 1-inch chunk of board added to each side where the eyebrow bone will stick out. A smaller head will require just the three 2-inch layers. If your horse will have a dramatic, windblown mane that sticks out more than usual on the romance side (the side that faces the spectators), you might need to add a fourth 1- or 2-inch board in the mane area on the romance side.

For a Menagerie Animal:

How many layers of wood you need for a menagerie animal obviously depends on the kind of animal being carved. For a large head for some of the more popular animals, we've used the following amounts of wood:

Tiger: Six 2-inch boards
Lion (male): Ten 2-inch boards
Cat: Five 2-inch boards

Rabbit: Five 2-inch boards
Giraffe: Four 2-inch boards
Goat: Four 2-inch boards
Dog: Three 2-inch boards

To make your own determination, consult the animal-anatomy book to see how your animal's head compares in width to a horse head, and make an educated guess of how many wood layers you will need to laminate the head.

Once you have cut out your pieces, lightly sand the edges of each piece to remove any splinters of wood or rough areas that might interfere with gluing. We usually glue all the layers of an individual pattern piece together first, and then glue the laminated chunks together. Using your fingers or a paint spatula, spread a liberal amount of glue on the face of each layer to be glued, so that no dry areas are evident. Glue the pieces together.

Here is where you will run into your first problem. When you press the layers together, they are going to slide around, and, if you are not careful, they will set up crooked. Wait about five minutes (the point at which the glue usually starts to set up), and then use one of the two methods to keep your layers aligned. In the first method, clamp the pieces together so they can't move. In the second method, using a hammer, partially tap in several small finishing nails at an angle through the layers to stop each layer from sliding.

Even if you clamped or nailed the pieces together, check them after about five more minutes to make sure they haven't shifted somehow (because your clamps aren't tight enough, or because your nails didn't go deep enough). Follow the same procedure for making the neck blank. Let the blanks dry for several hours—longer if it is especially cold or humid.

PEGGING THE HEAD TO THE NECK

At Horsin' Around, we've found that it's easier to rough out and carve the head, neck, and mane if the head and neck are already assembled. Before

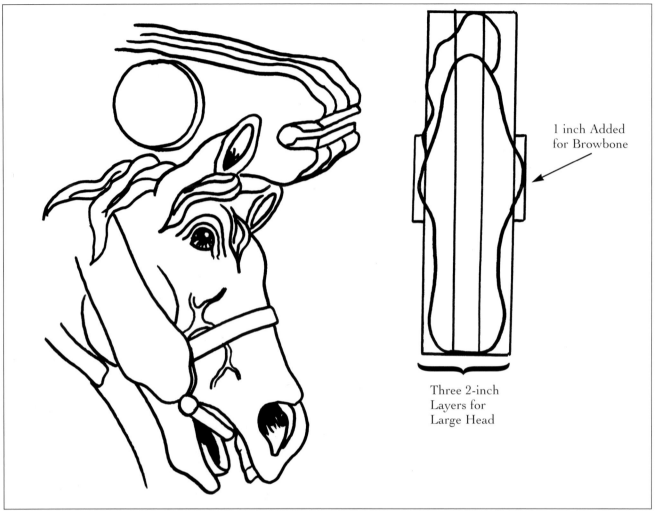

Illus. 8-1. **Laying out a pattern on planks to carve a horse's head.**

you glue the head and neck together, however, you need to peg them to make the joint stronger. We use 3/4-inch hardwood dowels for pegs. These dowels are available at any hardware store. You will also need a drill with a 3/4-inch spade bit, and 3/4-inch metal dowel centers (described in Chapter 2).

Begin by clamping the neck piece to a worktable, and hand-positioning the head on top of it. When the two are aligned (you might need an extra pair of hands to hold the head in place), draw a couple of alignment lines across and perpendicular to the head/neck joint on each side, to make it easier to line up the two pieces accurately after drilling the holes.

Next, drill two 2-inch-deep holes in the base of the neck, each one about 2 inches in from the end,

being careful to ensure that each hole is perpendicular to the plane of the base. (Note: If you don't have a drill guide to control the depth of the hole, use a piece of masking tape to mark the 2-inch line on the shaft of your drill.)

Next, place the metal dowel centers in the holes. Reposition the head on the neck, using the penciled alignment lines to accurately line up the two pieces. Using a mallet, tap the head onto the neck, so that the points of the dowel centers make an impression in the base of the head, indicating where you must drill the corresponding holes.

Now, remove the head from the neck. Clamp the head to the worktable, base up, and, using the marks from the metal dowel centers, drill the two corresponding 2-inch holes in the base of the head, again being careful to ensure that the holes are perpendicular to the plane of the base.

Cut two 3¾-inch lengths of dowel. Pour a little glue in the holes in the neck base, and place the dowels in the holes. Coat the surface of the neck base with glue. Then pour a little glue in the holes in the head base, and coat the head base with glue. Position the head on the neck. If you drilled the holes correctly, the two should line up. Clamp the head and neck together, or partially tap in small finishing nails at an angle to keep the two pieces from moving. Let the assembly dry for several hours.

Note: If you are carving a horse with what's called a "tucked head," which bends down and turns forward slightly, peg the head and neck but don't glue them together until you are done carving. It's difficult to carve parts of the tucked head while it is on the neck. You will also have to modify the neck area (and perhaps add on a little wood) to account for the turned head.

ROUGHING OUT THE HEAD AND NECK BLANK

When your head and neck blank is dry, remove the clamps or finishing nails. Using a black marker or thick lead pencil, draw on the top view of your horse head so that it looks similar to what is shown in Illus. 8-1. That will give you the basic shape of the head.

To reduce the head to a shape closer to the finished shape, use a large, shallow-sweep gouge and a mallet to carve away the excess wood (outside of your lines) in order to change the head from a squarish block to a horse-head shape.

To rough out the forelock—the part of the mane on the top of the head that falls forward—look at the photograph or pattern of the horse you are carving to determine the general shape and hair flow of the forelock, and then sketch that shape on the wood. Use a large, shallow-sweep gouge and a mallet to carve away the excess wood outside the lines. To rough out the neck at this point, just round off the corners.

Carving Techniques for Menagerie Animals:

If you are carving a menagerie animal instead of a horse, follow the same instructions above for cutting out, laminating, pegging, and gluing together the head and neck. To determine how to rough out your animal, look at the top-of-the-head view of your animal in an animal-anatomy book or on a three-dimensional model to get the general head shape. Sketch that shape on the top of your head blank. Then use a large, shallow-sweep gouge and a mallet to carve away the excess wood outside the lines. Use the same procedure for roughing out the neck.

DRAWING PROMINENT FACE AND NECK FEATURES AND TRAPPINGS

Now, take the pattern of the horse's head and place it on the romance side of your head blank. Slip some carbon paper (ink side towards the wood) between your pattern and the head blank. Then retrace the detail lines of your pattern to transfer the markings to the wood (Illus. 8-2). Unless you have really large carbon paper, you'll have to move the carbon paper around as you work. It will help to tape the pattern down in a few places to keep it from shifting.

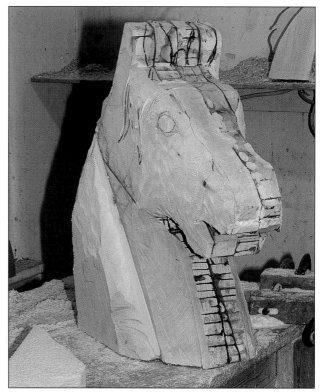

Illus. 8-2. **A roughed-out horse head with some markings transferred to it.**

When you have transferred all the lines of your pattern to the head, flip over both the head and your pattern, and transfer the same lines onto the other side of the head. (If you can't see the lines of your pattern through the paper when you flip it over, tape it to a window and trace the lines onto the back side of the pattern.)

When you have transferred all the lines, draw in any missing connecting lines, such as the strap across the top of the nose. When you are finished, you should have a wood-head blank with all the details drawn on it.

Ideally, all the lines you have transferred to the head blank should match the pattern (and thus the original animal) exactly. Since you are working with a lumpy piece of wood, however, lines that should be straight probably weren't transferred perfectly straight, and round circles probably weren't transferred perfectly round, etc. So at this point, it's a good idea to look at the markings on the wood and correct or redraw ones that you think will be a problem. For example, you can use a clear, flexible plastic ruler (found in office supply stores) to straighten up lines that should be relatively straight, such as on the straps. (The flexibility of the ruler will help you extend the straight lines across curved body parts.) You can use a compass to draw perfect circles right onto the wood. Correcting these small details so that they can be carved more accurately will enhance the quality of your carving.

Now, spend a few moments looking at the head blank, the photograph or pattern of the animal, and an anatomical drawing of the animal, noting how they correspond to each other. Stop looking at the head as a whole, and start visualizing it as a group of lines, curves, and three-dimensional layers.

Look at each detail, and note how it relates to other details. For example, if you are carving a horse, note that the straps stick out the farthest on the side of the head, followed by a D-shaped jawbone underneath the straps. Look at how the eyebrow bone protrudes, the nostrils flair, the lips, teeth, and tongue are positioned in relation to each other, and the chin narrows and ends up smaller than the upper part of the muzzle, ending in a kind of rounded knob. Note that the eyes are wider apart than the nostrils are. Once you feel reasonably familiar with how your head blank looks now and how it should look when you're done, you're ready to start carving.

FINDING THE ANIMAL IN THE WOOD

As we noted earlier, when asked how to carve a carousel animal, an old man once said, "Just carve away everything that isn't a carousel horse." That sounds simplistic, but basically reflects the philosophy you should use when carving your animal.

Before you start to carve, draw the centerline on top of the animal's head and down its mane or neck. Don't carve across that line unless it's unavoidable. If you are confused about a particular instruction, look at the photographs in the Carving Gallery for clarification. Also, be sure to securely clamp the head blank to a worktable before starting to carve.

Starting Point

You can begin anywhere you want in carving your head, but one good place to start is to round off most of the square edges. If you look at your photograph or pattern and a small plastic model, you'll see that there are very few square edges on a horse or any animal.

You should have removed much of the squareness in the roughing-out stage, but if you are inexperienced you were probably hesitant about roughing out as much as you could have. Using a medium-size gouge with a shallow sweep, round off the top edges of the muzzle, the front corners of the muzzle, the lower jaw, the bottom edge of the cheekbone, etc. Just shave down these areas; try not to let large chunks of wood splinter off. When you have rounded most of the edges, your blank will begin to take on more of the look of a real animal head.

Carving the Face

Most of our students start the detail carving of their animal head by carving the mouth area. Look at your photograph or pattern, and make sure you know which lines in the mouth area are the tongue, teeth, and lips. The lips will stick out the farthest, the next layer in will be the teeth, and the layer in from that will be the tongue if your horse has a visible one (Illus. 8-3).

If the area is not defined enough by the lines you transferred, look at your photograph and draw more lines to clarify the different areas of the mouth to be carved, and to indicate the wood that should remain and the wood that should be removed. Mark the high areas (the areas that will protrude the most); then identify the area of wood that should be removed completely, and put an X on it. If your animal has a bit going through its mouth, don't forget to leave wood in the back of the mouth in between the two outer circles of the bit. Then use a large or medium-size gouge with a shallow sweep and a mallet to carefully remove the X area.

Illus. 8-3. **A look at the detail on the face of a horse.**

Once the mouth area has the right overall shape, look at the mouths in the Carving Gallery and shape the different elements to make them look realistic. For example, round off the edges of the tongue, and make the top of it more flat and smooth. Flatten out the top and side edges of the teeth. (Don't make the ends of the teeth too thin, or they will break off. Also, note that the teeth angle outward.)

Horses have a canine tooth that is somewhat separate from the rest of the bottom teeth. If you want to put that in, carve out the space in between and shape that tooth. Flatten out the underside of the lips, and then round off the sides.

Next, you could carve the nostrils. Horse nostrils actually are more of a spiral than a circle, as shown in Illus. 8-3. Look carefully at your photograph to see how your horse's nostrils flare. If the lines you transferred in the nose area are not enough for you to define the area, look at your photograph and the photographs in the Carving Gallery and draw the features you need.

Begin carving the nostrils by using a V-parting tool or a small veiner and a mallet to make a groove along the inner line of your spiral. Carve out the underside of the top sweep of the spiral, so the top sweep of the nostril protrudes more than the inner sweep. The inner sweep will seem to fade into the nostril hole.

Using a medium-size gouge with a shallow sweep, start carving out a shallow hole inside the nostril outline. When you have a shallow hole, use a smaller gouge with a deep sweep (or a spoon gouge, if you have one) to hollow out a small, deeper hole in the back of the shallow hole, so it looks as if the small nostril hole bores into the head.

Next, use a medium veiner to carve out a small, rounded groove between the bottom of the nostril sweep and the top of the upper lip on each side. (The groove transitions into a flat area on the front of the nose.) This will leave both the upper lip and the nostril standing out. Round off the upper edge of the lip all the way around.

Carving the top of the head is a logical next step. If you look at the photographs in the Carving Gallery, you'll note that the bone on the top of the horse head forms a kind of square-bottomed V. The bottom of the V is between the nostrils, and the V opens up as it approaches the brow bones, which are the widest part of the head.

Remember that the very top of the head, where the centerline runs, is fine without any carving, except what you need to carve to make a strap across the nose stand up in relief. Draw the V-shaped bone on the wood. Then use a medium gouge with a medium sweep to carve out some of the area outside the lines of the V, using your photograph or model as a guide. Don't carve away too much, or the eye will be affected.

Next, you could move to the side of the head. First, use a V-parting tool to outline the edges of the strap lines you transferred or drew on. The strap has to protrude from the animal's head as a real one would, so leave the top face of the strap alone, and use a medium gouge with a shallow sweep to shave away the wood on both sides of the strap, until the strap is standing in relief about 1/8 of an inch. Do this with all straps.

If you have a ring on the straps, note that real straps will go over and through the ring, so your straps should be higher than the ring where the two meet. Photographs in the Carving Gallery show the position of the straps and the ring. Outline the outside and inside diameters of the ring, and carve away the excess wood to leave the ring in relief. The micro-carving tools can be useful in cleaning up the inside of the ring.

If the straps on your horse have decorations, look carefully at your photograph or pattern to see how the decorations relate to the straps—e.g., if they are higher or lower, overlapping, or even— and then carve them accordingly. If your horse has a bit going through its mouth, carve the two outer circles of the bit (one on each side of the mouth), and then round the bit inside the mouth to match the same curve of the circles.

At this point, you have to carve the D-shaped cheekbone. Look at the cheekbone in your photograph or pattern and the photographs in the Carving Gallery. The D-shaped cheekbone starts with the straight line of the D parallel to the strap just above the top edge of the strap. Then it circles under the strap to the bottom of the head and around to the point where the underside of the head meets the neck. Define the cheekbone by carving out the wood just outside the lines of the D, and then carve to taper the wood away from the D shape according to the anatomy of each part.

Many beginners have trouble shaping the bottom of the cheekbone, as well as the underside of the area just behind the mouth. This area should be rounded and should narrow as it goes down, rather than be square-sided with rounded corners. If you have trouble achieving this, try using a riffler file (described in Chapter 2) to get the result you want. Use the photographs in the Carving Gallery to determine the proper shape and angle of these areas.

Once you have shaped the cheekbone, you could move to the chin area. Look at your photograph or pattern and the photographs in the Carving Gallery. The chin is a knob centered underneath the mouth area. Part of it should already be shown protruding on the profile of the head. Draw a circle where the bottom of the chin knob should be. Then carve away from the circle to lower the wood around the knob, rounding the knob and tapering the chin area into the rest of the underside of the head.

Carving the Eye Area

The eye area consists of the brow bone, the eyelids, and the eyes themselves. When you transferred your pattern markings to your wood, you should have drawn where the eyes go. Review those markings before you start carving, to ensure they are accurate and that the eyes are in the same place on both sides of the head.

Before you carve the eye area, we recommend that you set the glass eyes. At Horsin' Around, we order glass eyes with a flat back from a taxidermy supply house. We use 27-millimeter eyes for a small animal, 29-millimeter eyes for a medium animal, and 31-34-millimeter eyes for a large animal.

To set it, first center the glass eye over the eye drawn on the wood and trace around it, so you know its exact shape and size. Then look at the top curve of the eye in your photograph or pattern, and draw a matching curved line about one quarter of the way down the traced eye circle on the wood to represent the upper eyelid. (If your animal has a lowered lid, lower the line to match your photograph or pattern.)

Next, carve a shallow hole inside the traced eye circle, up to the point of the curved line of the eyelid. The hole should be angled slightly inward at its front, so the eye will face slightly forward instead of looking straight out the side of the head.

Now, carve out a shallow area under the upper eyelid up to the upper edge of the eye circle, so the eye can be inserted under the eyelid. Insert the eye into the hole to check its fit and position, and modify your hole as needed. When the eye fits and is positioned correctly, put a little glue on the back of the eye and glue it into the hole.

The next step is to mix some carveable wood putty to seal up the crack around the eye. Put a little putty on your finger, and run your finger around the perimeter of the eye, until the putty fills the crack. Immediately wet a rag and wipe off any putty you inadvertently smeared on the eye; then let the putty dry. When it is dry, cover the glass eye with tape to keep your gouges from scratching it as you finish shaping the eye area.

Now, carve the area outside the eye to give it the proper shape. Draw a small tear duct in the front corner of the eye, and use a small gouge or micro-carving tool to shape it. Then use the same tool to outline the line of the lower lid. Look at the Carving Gallery for some close-up detail photographs of eye areas for guidance.

Next, look at your photograph or pattern to see how to shape the brow-bone area. Bear in mind as you carve the brow bone that it is the widest area of the horse's head, and from that point the head narrows progressively to a thin strip at the back. Since this thin strip is where the mane originates, it is often masked by the flow of the mane, particularly on wood horses. Carve the top of the upper eyelid up under the brow bone to match the angles and shape of your photograph or pattern.

Carving the Veins

Many carousel horses had prominent veins carved into their faces, as shown in Illus. 8-3. The veins add some realism, but not all the horses displayed them, so you don't have to carve them if you prefer not to. If you choose to carve them, look at your photograph and the photographs in the Carving Gallery to see what they look like when carved. Then draw the veins on both sides of the horse head. Since the veins are very subtle and protrude only slightly from the face, you need to use a light touch when you carve them.

Using a small gouge with a deep sweep, very lightly carve a very shallow groove just outside the lines of the veins, so the veins stand up slightly in relief. Then use a shallow-sweep gouge to lightly carve away the outside edge of the groove (away from the vein) so it blends smoothly into the rest of the face.

Carving the Ears

Ears on carousel horses usually point the same way and are symmetrical (in other words, they match each other). But some carvers varied them to show expression, such as fear, attentiveness, meanness, or even defeat. Illus. 8-4 shows some of the different styles of ears. Look at your photograph or pattern, an anatomy book, any models you have, and the Carving Gallery to familiarize yourself with the general shape of horse ears and to get a feel for the high and low areas.

Because you have produced your blueprint (and thus your wood blank) from a side view of the animal, the ears should be sticking up the right way in profile, but they will be part of one continuous block of wood across the top of the head. A good place to start carving the ears is to draw the shape of the outside of each ear (and the line across the head between the two ears, where the forelock flows between them) on the ear area, and mark with an X the area of wood between the ears that has to be removed. Remove that wood with a large gouge and a mallet. Once that wood is gone, the outside of the ears will be closer to their proper shape.

Next, look at your photograph and other references again and round the outside of the ears until they match the examples. Note that the outsides of the ears are convex, but that there is a small, slightly concave curve near the top of the inside edges of the ears. Also pay attention to the way the ears come to a point, and carve accordingly. (Avoid making the ear points too sharp and thin, so they don't break off.)

Now, draw the detail lines on the inside of the ears, to mark the outer ring of cartilage and the hole where the ear canal recedes into the head. Carve out the inside of the ear area, tapering it from a shallow area at the tip and gradually getting deeper as you approach the inside bottom. (If you're carving your animal over an extended period of time, you might want to wait to completely carve the inside of the ear. Leaving it thick will make it less likely to be broken off if the head inadvertently gets knocked over.) Using a veiner or a spoon gouge, dig out a small hole to reflect the opening of the ear canal.

Carving the Mane

The mane seems intimidating at first for many inexperienced carvers, but they usually find that it's one of the most fun parts to carve because it offers a chance to be creative. Before you start, spend a little time looking at the mane in the photograph or pattern of your animal, and in the photographs in the Carving Gallery. Note that the strands of hair that make up manes always flow over and under other strands in a kind of rolling motion, and that manes are usually made up of locks of varying lengths and thickness that angle 30-45 degrees across the neck.

On American carousel horses, the mane also always falls across the horse on the romance (right) side. (The left side of the horse usually displays a bare neck, or perhaps just a few short locks draped over it for effect. See the Carving Gallery for a photograph of the left side of a horse.) Exceptions to this are when the mane is flowing straight back as if the horse were in a fast gallop, or when the mane is "roached" (cut short so it stands straight up, as shown in Illus. 8-5).

Next, you have to draw in some mane details. First, make sure the lines of the outer edges where the mane meets the neck are drawn in. You should

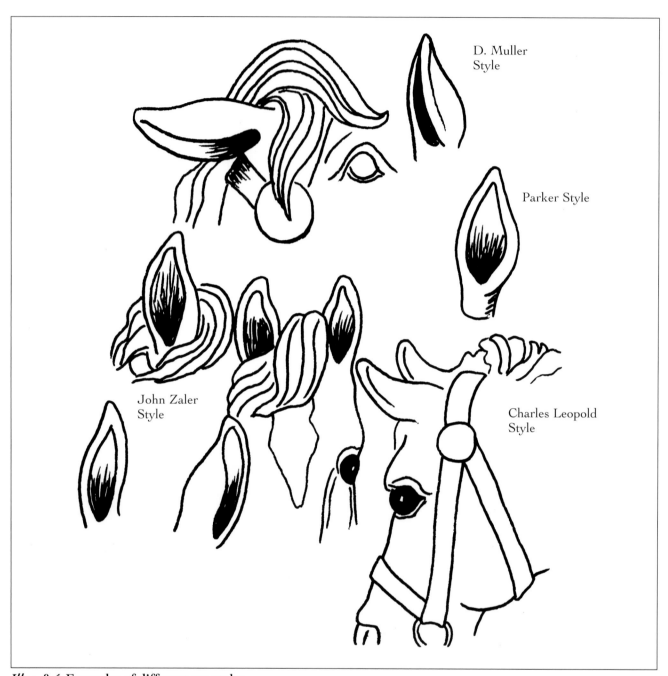

Illus. 8-4. **Examples of different ear styles.**

have transferred these from your pattern, but if they aren't clear enough, redraw them.

Now, pick out the major definition lines (the biggest, most prominent hair locks) of the mane in your photograph(s). Then identify those same lines on your wood. (If they are not there, draw them in.) Once you identify them, you may want to highlight the major mane lines on your wood by drawing them thicker, and shade the hair locks so they stand out visually. Since you can't see the

mane on the back of the head in the side-view photograph or pattern of your animal, you will have to imagine how the lines of the prominent hair locks extend around the back of the head and draw them accordingly.

The first step to carving the mane is to use the V-parting tool to outline the outer edges of the mane where it touches the neck. Leave the mane high, and use a shallow-sweep gouge to shave down the neck area slightly so the edges of the mane stand out in relief. The outer edges of the mane will not stand out much, usually, since the tips of the hair are relatively thin, although there are exceptions.

Illus. 8-5. A "roached" mane.

Next, using your V-parting tool again, outline the lines of the prominent hair locks, going over each groove several times to achieve deep, dramatic cuts. In between the prominent hair locks, carve off a thin layer of wood so the prominent locks stand out in relief. Now your mane is, in a fashion, defined.

Remember, as we noted above, that most manes are made up of locks of varying lengths and thickness that angle at roughly 30-45 degrees across the neck. You might find it useful at this point to draw in minor detail lines that follow the flow of the prominent hair locks, but end at different points and vary in thickness. Look at your photograph or pattern for guidance. You can then outline the minor detail lines with the V-parting tool.

Since every mane is so different, we can't tell you specifically how to carve your mane from this point on. Basically, you will carve lines and grooves of varying heights, depths, widths, and lengths. We can, however, give you some pointers to help you get a good result:

1. Use the veiner gouges if possible, because they work better for manes.

2. Constantly change the size of your gouge, if possible, so that the strands vary in size.

3. Make sure the different locks are not all the same shape. Manes are somewhat wild-looking, so you don't want a great deal of symmetry or sameness.

4. Vary the depths of cut. The pieces of the mane have to be of different heights and depths to appear realistic and have the appropriate dramatic effect.

5. Don't worry about following precisely your detail lines. One of the fun things about manes is that there is so much variety. If when you carve a line you think it might be better to curve it differently than you've drawn it, do so. And if you make what you consider to be a mistake, don't worry about it. Often a mistake that has been recarved into a different shape or flow ends up being one of the best elements of your mane, because it's more original than what you could have imagined in the first place. The Carving Gallery presents several examples of interesting manes.

6. As always in carving, keep your tools sharp. Keeping the cuts in your mane clean will make the mane look better and save you sanding time later.

Carving the Forelock

If your horse has a forelock, your main goal in carving it will be to make the forelock match the mane in style and flow. Follow the same procedures in carving it that you used for the mane. Find the edges and the prominent locks, and outline them with a V-parting tool. Draw in your minor detail lines, and outline them. Then carve in the lines and grooves of varying heights, depths, widths, and lengths.

Carving the Neck

The neck is one area where a plastic model and a good animal-anatomy book really come in handy, because carving the neck is all about knowing the anatomy of the animal. Look at Illus. 8-6 and the photographs in the Carving Gallery, and draw the muscles on the neck. Use a medium-size or large gouge with a shallow sweep to carve the gentle slopes and curves of the neck until they match the examples. Don't do much shaping at the bottom of the neck. You will have to wait to carve that area when you assemble your horse, so you can carve the transition of the neck into the chest area on the body.

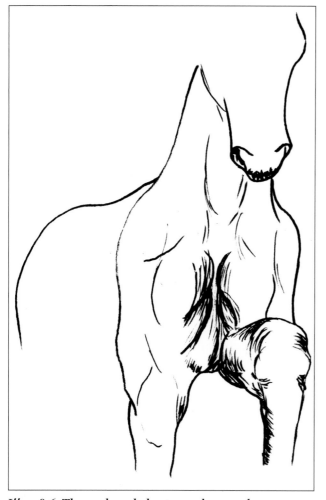

Illus. 8-6. **The neck and chest muscles on a horse.**

CARVING TECHNIQUES FOR MENAGERIE ANIMAL CARVERS

All the carving instructions presented above can apply to menagerie animals. The key to carving your animal successfully is knowing what it looks like in three dimensions. Since most menagerie animals do not have trappings on their heads, you will simply need to concentrate on their anatomical features. Begin by defining the bone and muscle structure, determining what is high (what protrudes the most)

and what is low. Work on getting the overall shape right before you start refining the details.

One thing you might encounter that someone carving a horse won't is the carving of fur or skin texture. To figure out how your animal's fur or skin should be carved, look closely at the photograph of your animal. Is the fur or skin finely detailed? Does it have a direction of flow? Is the detail defined by lines, grooves, or pieces of fur or skin that protrude? Are the lines, grooves, or pieces of fur or skin short, long, or mixed?

If the fur or skin is carved with distinct lines, a V-parting tool will probably give you the effect that you want. If it is carved with grooves, a veiner might be your best tool choice. If pieces of fur or skin protrude, you will have to define the outline of each piece with a V-parting tool, and then carve out some area around the pieces with whatever tool will do the trick. If it will help, draw lines on your wood to guide you.

If you are uncertain how to get the look you want, find a scrap piece of wood and experiment with different tools and cuts. One important thing to remember is that-unlike some other aspects of the animal-with fur and skin and such surfaces as feathers, you are trying to achieve an artistic effect that *suggests* the real thing, not produce an accurate carved copy of the real thing. Judge the effect by stepping back from the animal and viewing it as someone admiring your finished animal would. Don't judge what it looks like when it is 4 inches from your face.

COMMON CARVING MISTAKES

Over the years at Horsin' Around, we have noticed that beginners tend to make some of the same mistakes. Here are some common mistakes to avoid when carving the head and neck:

1. Don't make the nostrils flare too dramatically, or the nose will look cartoonish.

2. Don't set the eyes in flat. Set the eyes inward at the front corners, so they look forward slightly rather than straight out to the side.

3. Don't make the locks of the mane too rounded, or the mane will look like it has worms instead of hair locks.

4. Don't leave the ears too thick. Hollow out the ears appropriately, so they don't look like chunks perched atop the head.

CARVING GALLERY

Illus. 8-7 to 8-33 are close-up photographs of carousel animals that show different carved features of the head, neck, and mane that you can refer to when carving. *The Carving Gallery photos were taken by Thomas L. Cory.*

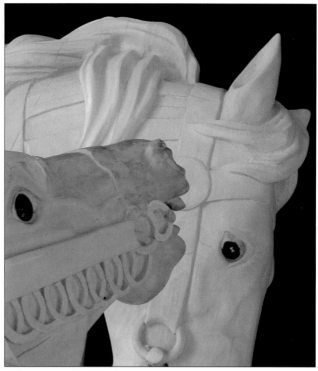

Illus. 8-7. The rear horse head is an example of a tucked head.

Illus. 8-8. The dramatic mane on the replica of this Daniel Mueller Indian pony is carved to flow straight back as if the pony is galloping.

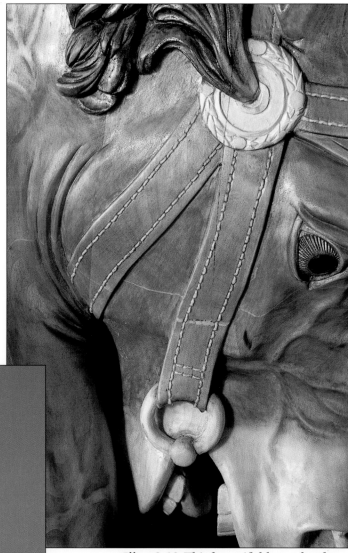

Illus. 8-9.

Illus. 8-10. This beautiful horse has been carved to be extremely realistic, with highly defined veins on the face and emphasized folds of skin on the neck.

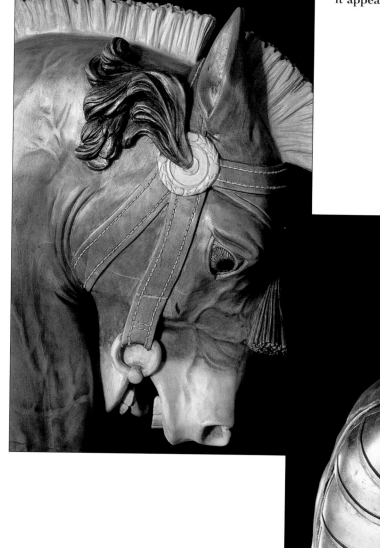

Illus. 8-11. The mane on this horse is roached, which means it appears to have been clipped to about 2 or 3 inches.

Illus. 8-12. The trappings on this ornate horse have been carved to emulate medieval armor, the protective coverings that were worn in battle.

Illus. 8-13.

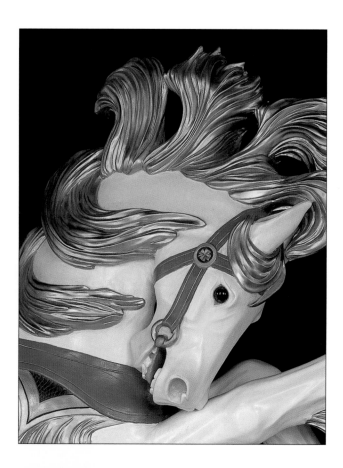

Illus. 8-14. A Horsin' Around carver works on his horse's forelock, the part of the mane falling forward on top of the head.

Illus. 8-15.

Illus. 8-16. This horse head has been carved with a wonderfully gentle expression.

Illus. 8-17. The peaceful mane on this horse is a good match for the placid expression on its face.

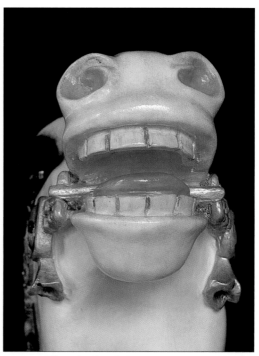

Illus. 8-18. It's important to carve the two sides of the head so they are basically symmetrical, as shown here.

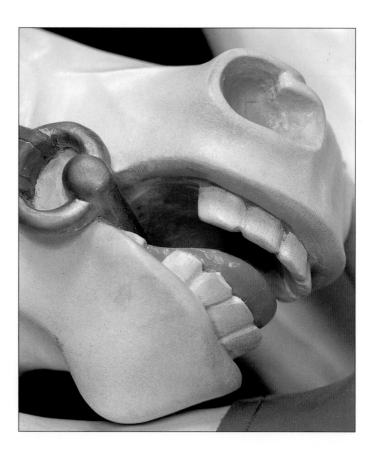

Illus. 8-19. The horse head shown here has a realistically carved face: spiral nostrils, teeth angled slightly outward, tongue slightly curved, and bit in the back of the mouth.

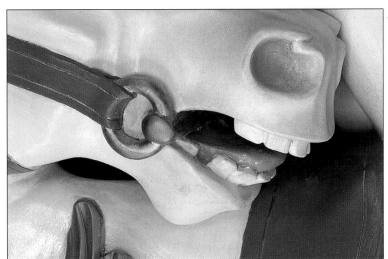

Illus. 8-20.

Illus. 8-21. **This close-up of an Indian pony shows the feathers and other trappings that grace the neck and head areas.**

Illus. 8-22. This finely carved eye gets its expression from its angled shape and well-defined eyelids.

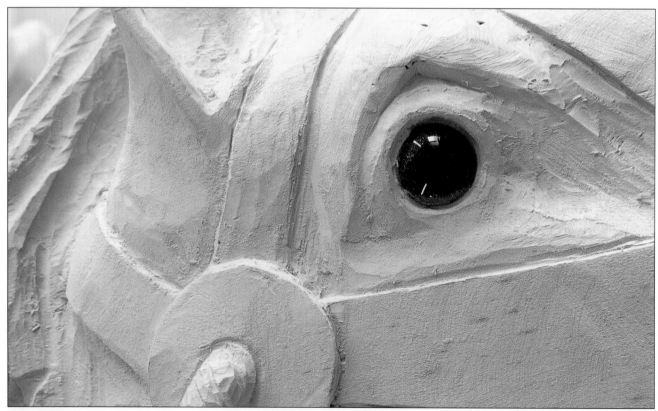

Illus. 8-23. The eye on this horse is carved more simply that the one shown in Illus. 8-22, but still has an expression all its own.

Illus. 8-24. The ears on this Indian pony are angled flat back, consistant with the posture and attitude of its head and body.

Illus. 8-25. The ear on this horse is nicely shaped with a slight knob, a pointed tip, and a hollowed-out inside.

Illus. 8-26. The nonromance side of this horse shows a well-defined neck.

Illus. 8-27. As is characteristic on carousel horses, the mane on this horse drapes dramatically over the romance side.

Illus. 8-28. This view of the nonromance side of the horse in Illus. 8-27 shows how little mane is showing on the left side of the neck.

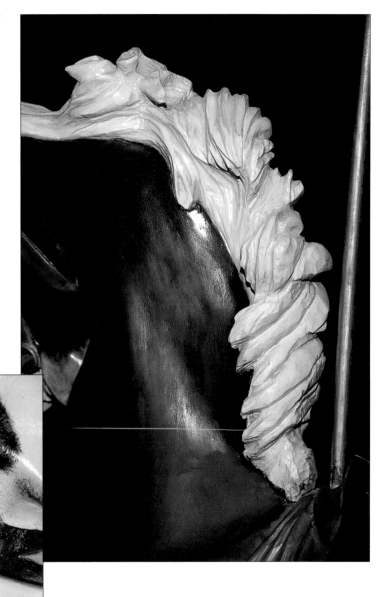

Illus. 8-29. The trappings on the head of this Indian pony have intricately carved feathers, beads, and jewels.

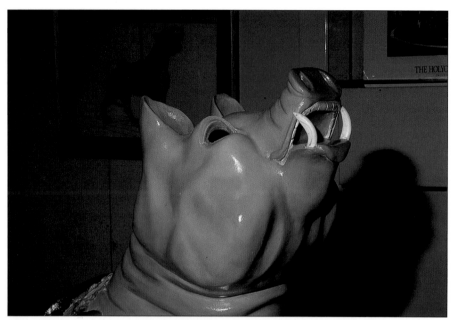

Illus. 8-30. This Dentzel-style pig has tusks, but still has a friendly expression.

Illus. 8-31. This fanciful frog, similar in style to an original Herschell-Spillman Company frog, has a delightful face.

Illus. 8-32. Ostrich.

Illus. 8-33. Giraffe.

9

Preparing and Carving the Tail

If you are carving a horse, it's decision time: Are you going to carve the tail out of wood or buy a real horsehair tail? It's purely a matter of choice, but you do need to take into consideration the style of your horse when making the decision. For example, if you're carving a dramatic galloping horse, with the mane streaming straight out from the back of the head, a real horsehair tail that sedately drapes down the rump will not look as if it belongs on that horse. Conversely, if you are carving a horse with a peaceful stance and a wispy, draping mane, a real horsehair tail will look just right-and may even add a certain elegance. This chapter describes how to carve your own tail as well as how to install a real horsehair tail.

MAKING THE CARVING BLANK

If you are carving a wood tail, the first thing you need to do is modify your tail pattern. On your full-size blueprint, the tail section ends where it meets the body. When it's time to assemble your animal, however, the tail needs to have an extension of wood that can be inserted into a hole on the body, as shown in Illus. 9-1. To account for the extension, cut out the tail pattern. Then trace it on a longer piece of paper and extend the lines where the tail meets the body by about 4 inches. Cut out the new pattern.

Next, you need to determine how many layers of wood have to be laminated to give the tail its needed width. If your blueprint calls for a tail that sticks straight out and then drapes down, two 2-inch layers should be adequate. However, if your animal has a tail that is very full in width or one that curls forward around the hind leg on the romance side (see Illus. 9-1), you will most likely need to laminate three 2-inch layers.

Once you know how many layers you need, trace the pattern pieces twice (or three times) onto the wood. If the arch of your tail makes it too wide to fit on one plank, line up two planks and trace

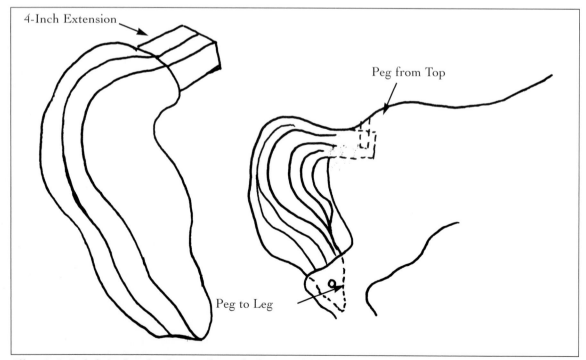

Illus. 9-1. At left is the glued-up and roughed-out tail blank. The drawing on the right shows how to install the carved tail.

the pattern across the two. Cut out each piece with a band saw, and then sand the edges a bit to remove any splintered areas that might interfere with gluing.

Next, determine which surfaces will be glued together, coat each surface with glue, and glue the pieces together. After about five minutes, clamp the pieces together or partially tap in a couple of finishing nails at an angle through the layers so the pieces don't shift and set up crooked. Let the pieces dry for several hours, or longer if the weather is especially cold or humid. If you divided the tail into two pieces, glue up the two laminated chunks to make a whole tail.

ROUGHING OUT THE TAIL BLANK

When the tail blank is dry, remove the clamps or finishing nails. Look at the photograph or pattern of your animal, and think about how the tail would look if you were viewing it from the top down, and from the back. As you can see in the Carving Gallery that appears at the end of this chapter, most carousel horse tails roll over and under on the romance side.

Using a black marker or thick lead pencil, draw the top view of the outline of your tail, and then draw the back view of the outline, as shown in Illus. 9-2. Remember that the centerline goes down the topside of the tail, so the profile view of the tail should be relatively accurate without carving. To help remove excess wood and get your tail reduced to a shape closer to the finished shape, use a large, shallow-sweep gouge and mallet to carve away the excess wood (outside of your lines) in order to change the tail to the shape you want.

DRAWING THE TAIL'S FLOW ON THE BLANK

The most important thing to keep in mind when defining the tail is that it should be compatible with the mane, both in style and position. For example, if the mane is wispy and has delicate, draping locks, make the tail wispy with delicate, draping locks. This is the reason we recommend that you carve the tail right after carving the head, since carving the tail is basically an extension of carving the mane.

To draw the flow of the tail on the wood, first pick out the major definition lines (the biggest,

most prominent hair locks) of the tail in your photograph or pattern. Then identify those same lines on your wood, or draw them on if they're not there. Once you identify them, you may want to highlight the lines on your wood by drawing them thicker, and shade the hair locks so they stand out visually. Since you can't see the back of the tail in the side-view photograph or pattern of your animal, you will have to imagine how the lines of the prominent hair locks extend around the back of the tail and draw them accordingly.

FINDING THE ANIMAL IN THE WOOD

The first step to carving the tail is to use the V-parting tool to outline the lines of the prominent hair locks, going over each groove several times to achieve deep, dramatic cuts. In between the prominent hair locks, use a medium gouge with a shallow sweep to carve off a thin layer of wood so the prominent locks stand out in relief.

As with the mane, you might find it useful at this point to draw in minor detail lines that follow the flow of the prominent hair locks, but end at different points and vary in thickness. Look at your photograph or pattern for guidance. You can then outline the minor detail lines with the V-parting tool.

From this point on, you need to carve the details of the tail using the same technique and types of cuts that you used to carve the mane. You don't want the mane and tail to be identical, but they should look as if they belong on the same horse. All the tips for carving the mane apply to the tail. One of them bears repeating here: Keep your tools sharp. Ensuring that the cuts in the tail are clean will make the tail look better and save you sanding time later.

CARVING TECHNIQUES FOR MENAGERIE ANIMAL CARVERS

Since animals have such different styles of tails, the photograph or pattern of your animal, an animal-anatomy book, and a good plastic model will be your best aids in carving the tail for your animal. As with the horse tail, you will first need to modify your pattern to create the extension that is inserted into a hole on the body. If your animal has a small tail that is not very heavy, you can make the extension somewhat shorter, or perhaps even use a dowel to peg the tail to the body. Use your best judgment.

When you are ready to cut the pieces out, it should be fairly easy to estimate how many layers you need to laminate in order to make the tail. After gluing up the tail blank, draw the outline shape of the tail, and then carve away the excess wood to rough it out. If you are uncertain how to carve the proper texture (such as fur), experiment with different tools and cuts on a piece of scrap wood until you find a technique that works.

INSTALLING A HORSEHAIR TAIL

Though we're presenting the instructions for installing the tail in this chapter, be aware that installing a horsehair tail is the very last step in completing your horse, after the painting and final coats of clear finish. Working with the tail is relatively easy, if you follow a few simple steps. It's helpful for positioning if you have a photograph of a carousel horse with a real horsehair tail to use as a guide.

When you buy a horsehair tail, the horsehide it is attached to will either be flat or rolled. You have to soften the horsehide and reshape it before attaching it to your horse. The best way to soften the horsehide is to immerse it in a gallon of water with four tablespoons of powdered bleach stirred in, and let it soak for a day or two. When the hide is soft, remove it from the bleach water and hang it up until it quits dripping, but is still damp.

Now, find a piece of scrap wood and shape it to make a curved tail plug about 10 inches long, 4 inches wide, and 2 inches high, as shown in Illus. 9-2. Spread some wood glue on the plug. Then center the horsehide piece on the wood at the body end of the plug, and nail or staple it in the middle to anchor it. Next, *tightly* wrap one side of the horsehide around the plug, and nail or staple it in place. Then tightly wrap the other side of the horsehide around the plug, and nail or staple it.

To install the tail, hold the end of the plug up to the rump at the point where it will be attached. (This point is fairly high; look at your photograph for guidance.) Trace around the plug on the rump, so you know how big a hole you will need to make to insert it. Using a drill, drill out some of the wood on the inside of the traced area. Then chisel out the rest until the hole is the shape of the plug and about 4 inches deep. Then insert the tail plug, using a dowel and mallet to tap it tightly in place.

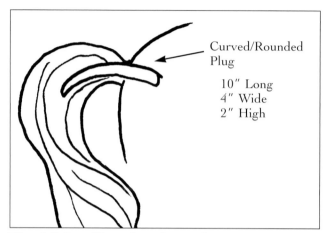

Curved/Rounded Plug

10" Long
4" Wide
2" High

Illus. 9-2. **Installing a horsehair tail.**

If you want to shape the tail, you can soak the whole tail rather than just the horsehide, and then shape it after you install it but before it dries. To shape the tail into a graceful drape, prop up the part of the tail that should arch with a piece of padded board. Then lightly bind the draping hair at several points, so that it falls in a natural line. Wait until the tail is completely dry before removing the board and ties.

One last note: Even though you will install the tail after painting, we recommend you order the tail *before* painting the animal, so that you can take into consideration the color of the real tail when choosing the other colors of your animal.

COMMON CARVING MISTAKES

Here are some common mistakes to avoid when carving the tail:

1. Don't carve the tail in a style that differs radically from the style of the mane.

2. Don't make the locks too rounded, or they will look like worms rather than hair locks.

3. Don't make the tail curve in the wrong direction. If it curves, it should curve around the romance side of the animal.

CARVING GALLERY

Illus. 9-3 to 9-11 show close-ups of several carved tails that you can refer to when carving. Since carving the tail uses the same techniques as carving the mane, also refer to the mane photographs in the Carving Gallery in Chapter 8. *The Carving Gallery photos were taken by Thomas L. Cory.*

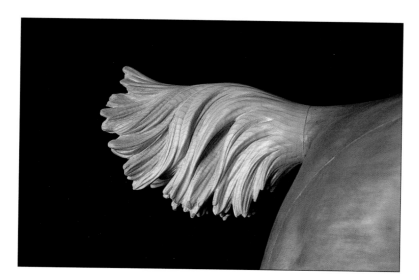

Illus. 9-3. The cropped tail on this horse has a wonderful sense of movement.

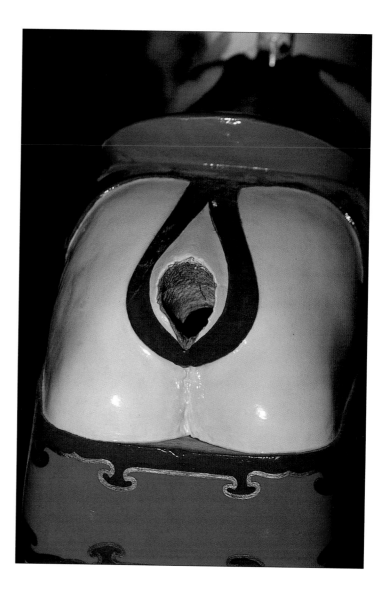

Illus. 9-4. As shown on this horse, the hole for the tail plug is drilled fairly high on the rump.

Illus. 9-5. This Indian pony has a very full, spread-out tail to match the wildness of its expression and posture.

Illus. 9-6. The tail on this horse has a nice drape to it, similar to the drape of the mane.

Illus. 9-7. Tails should curve around and towards the romance side, as shown on this tiger, and should be pegged unobtrusively to the leg if they are heavy and in danger of snapping off.

Illus. 9-8. The cropped tail on this stander (shown close up in Illus. 9-3) is very well suited to it.

Illus. 9-9. It's important to carve the tail in the same style as the mane, as shown on this stander.

Illus. 9-10. An upturned tail is just right on this playful zebra, similar to an original Herschell-Spillman zebra.

Illus. 9-11. Giraffes and other animals have very different styles of tails than horses, so check photographs and anatomy books before carving a menagerie animal tail.

10

Preparing and Carving the Legs

Compared to carving the head and body, carving the legs would seem to be very easy. But the legs can be a little tricky. In fact, some beginning carvers say they are one of the hardest parts to carve accurately. If you take it step by step, however, and pay attention to the anatomy of the animal, you should have no problem.

MAKING CARVING BLANKS

The first thing you need to do is cut out the leg patterns from the blueprint, dividing each leg at the pattern cutting lines. If you have two legs that overlap on your blueprint, you have to make an extra copy of the partially covered leg and draw in the missing lines.

Before you cut the wood, remember a few important points. Always lay out the leg patterns so the wood grain runs the length of the leg. That will make the legs stronger. If your animal is a stander and you corrected the stance on your blueprint as instructed in Chapter 3, your patterns should be accurate. If you skipped that step, go back to those instructions and correct the stance now, or you will spend a lot of time trying to even up each leg during assembly so that your animal can stand.

Once your pattern is corrected, make sure each wood piece you cut out accurately matches your pattern. Two 2-inch layers are sufficient for laminating the leg blank.

Trace the leg patterns onto the wood, tracing two identical layers for each part of each leg. If you have a leg that is straight, it does not need to be divided into upper and lower parts. Cut out each piece using the band saw, marking the pieces as you cut them out—such as "upper hind leg left" and "lower front leg right"—so you don't get the pieces mixed up. Then sand the edges a bit to get rid of any splintered areas that might interfere with gluing.

Next, glue the matching pieces together. After about five minutes, clamp the pieces together or

partially tap in a couple of finishing nails at an angle through the layers so the pieces don't shift and set up crooked. (Instead of using finishing nails, you can use handy things called "pinch dogs," shown in Illus. 10-1, which are available in woodworking catalogs.) Repeat this process for each of the leg chunks. Let the pieces dry for several hours—longer if the weather is especially cold or humid.

When the pieces are dry, level the knee-joint surfaces of the two-part legs using a planer or a sander. Then glue the pieces together to make whole legs. After about five minutes, clamp the pieces together for each leg or partially tap in a couple of finishing nails at an angle through the layers so the pieces don't shift and set up crooked.

Once you have all your leg pieces glued up, you can pile up a number of them vertically and clamp them all together. Let the pieces dry for several hours—longer if the weather is especially cold or humid.

To make your horse look natural, you must add a little more wood to the inner thigh area of the legs. Look at Illus. 10-1, and cut out a piece of 1-inch-thick wood to cover an area on your horse leg about the same size and proportion as shown in the illustration. Position the 1-inch block of wood on the leg, and trace around it so you know where to put glue on the leg. Glue the block to the wood, clamp or nail them together, and let the assembly dry for several hours—longer if the weather is especially cold or humid. Repeat this process for all the legs.

PEGGING THE LEGS AT THE KNEES

When the leg blanks are dry, remove all clamps or finishing nails. At Horsin' Around, we've found that it's safer to peg the two-part legs at the knees before carving, because it's less likely they will break. You'll need 1/2-inch hardwood dowels for pegs, and a drill with a 1/2-inch spade bit.

Begin by clamping the leg to a worktable, with

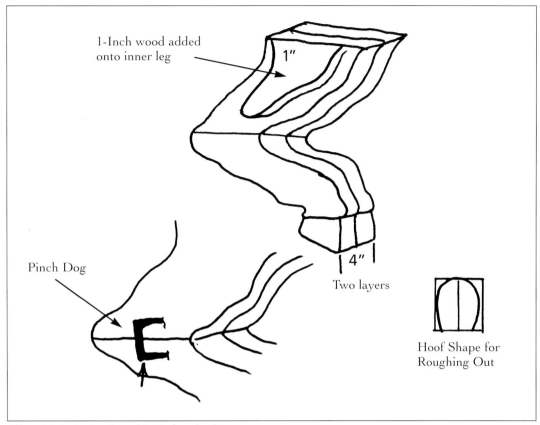

Illus. 10-1. **A glued-up block for the leg.**

the knee facing you. Drill two 1/2-inch holes through the knee area so each hole starts in one half of the leg and continues into the other half. Pour some glue into the holes, and then insert pieces of dowel that are a little longer than the holes are deep. Then saw or carve off the ends of the dowels so they're flush with the knee surface.

ROUGHING OUT THE LEG BLANKS

Using a black marker or thick lead pencil, draw on the front view of your horse leg with a black marker, so that it looks similar to the drawing shown in Illus. 10-2. That will give you the basic shape of the leg. Then turn the leg on its end, and draw the hoof's shape on the bottom of the leg, as shown in Illus. 10-1.

Next, turn the leg on its other end, and draw the shape of the top of the thigh, as shown in Illus. 10-3. Repeat the process for all the legs. To help remove excess wood and get your leg reduced to a shape closer to the finished shape, use a large, shallow-sweep gouge and mallet to carve away the excess wood (outside of your lines) in order to change each leg from a squarish block to a proper leg shape.

Carving Techniques for Menagerie Animal Carvers

If you are carving a menagerie animal instead of a horse, follow the same instructions above for cutting out, laminating, gluing, and pegging the legs of your animal. To determine how to rough out your animal, look at the front and back views of your animal's legs in an animal-anatomy book (or on a three-dimensional model) to get the general shape. Sketch that shape on the legs. Then use a large, shallow-sweep gouge and mallet to carve away the excess wood outside the lines.

DRAWING PROMINENT LEG FEATURES ON THE BLANK

Many original carousel horses showed little bone or muscle definition in their legs. Daniel Muller's carvings were an exception, in that they displayed wonderfully realistic leg detail. At Horsin' Around,

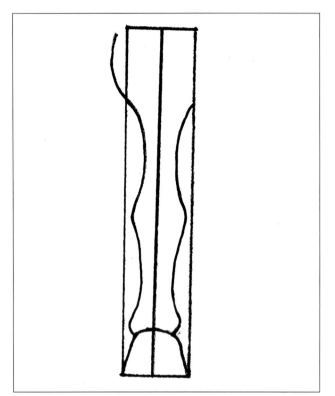

Illus. 10-2. **The shape of the leg is drawn on the wood for roughing out.**

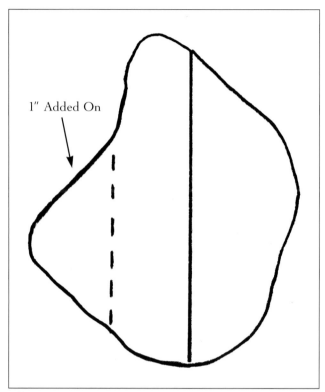

1" Added On

Illus. 10-3. **Cross-section of the top of the leg, showing 1-inch wood added to the inner thigh.**

most of the carvers like to include some definition, because they feel it gives the legs a better look. If you want to make your animal's legs relatively realistic, you will need to draw the basic muscle and bone structure on the blank.

Look at the leg drawings in Illus. 10-4 and the photographs in the Carving Gallery. The first thing you need to note about horse legs is that the front legs bend backward at the knee and the back legs bend forward at the knee. This results in some differences in the upper half of the legs, and in the knees. Below the knee, all four legs are basically the same, except that the back legs show the back tendon a little more prominently. Note that the outside of the upper leg has a prominent muscle showing, which is smooth and supple.

The knee area is similar to a round ball, with slightly flat sides. When you look at the knee from the side, you'll notice that it is made up of two bones that meet, with a shallow groove between them. From the knee down, the leg narrows to become the cannon. The cannon has several thin tendons that show subtly on the sides (as shown in Illus. 10-5), the most prominent of which is about the width of a pencil on a full-size carousel horse.

The leg flares out again at the fetlock, which is also somewhat like a round ball, but has a knobby bone that protrudes in the back and a tuft of hair that points down. The fetlock curves in at the pastern. Then the leg flares out once again to form the coronet, which overhangs the hoof a bit. On the back of the leg, a narrow tendon protrudes almost the full length of the leg.

Once you understand the anatomy of the leg, draw the lines on your animal's legs to match the photographs and patterns you have. If your animal has a leg or legs that are bent, look at your photograph or pattern, an anatomy book, and Illus. 10-4 to see how the muscles change shape or position as the leg changes position. Draw your lines accordingly.

Some carvers like to carve the horseshoes, while others like to buy metal shoes to attach. If you want to carve your horseshoes, draw a line on the bottom of the hoof, about 3/8 of an inch up from the bottom. If you want to include the clip of the horseshoe, draw a small hump at the top front of the shoe.

FINDING THE ANIMAL IN THE WOOD

Before you start to carve the leg, there are a few

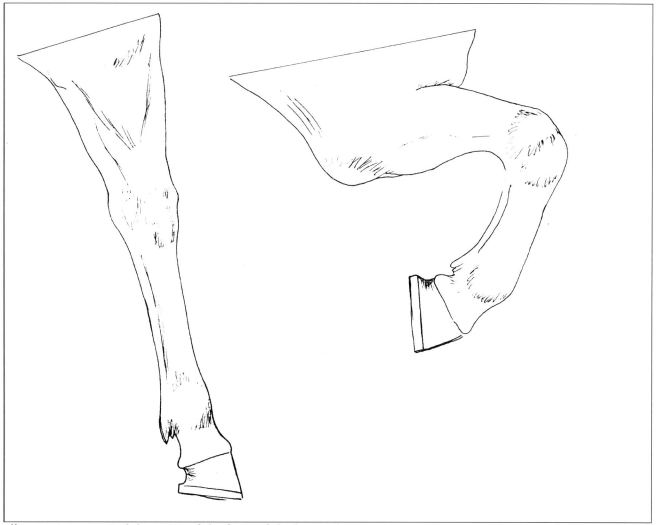

Illus. 10-4. **Anatomical drawings of the front of the horse's legs.**

important things you have to consider. First, whether you are carving legs with little detail or legs with fine detail, your most important goal—after shaping them correctly—is to make sure they match. You don't want one front knee to be 3 inches wide and the other to be 4 inches wide, or one leg to have bulging tendons and another to have tendons you can barely see. The legs don't have to be precise carbon copies of each other, but they do need to look as if they belong on the same animal. Decide how detailed you want them to be, and then carve them all the same way.

You don't want to carve the upper legs at this point, other than doing some very general shaping. Since the upper leg attaches to the body, wait until you have assembled your animal to finish carving that area, so you can carve a natural transition from leg to body. You can do more shaping

on the lower legs, but try not to overcarve them.

Horses' legs are relatively delicate for an animal of their size, but you don't want the legs to be too spindly. Leave them on the fat side; then you can finish carving them after you have carved the body and can compare the two to determine precise proportioning.

Remember that since you made your blank from a side-view photograph or drawing, the centerline could be extended down the front and back of your animal's legs. In other words, the profile (at the centerline) of your leg blanks will be very close to the proper proportion without any carving.

Do not make the pastern area too thin from front to back. If you feel as if you might be in danger of splitting off wood in that area by mistake, try using a riffler file to shape the back of the pastern.

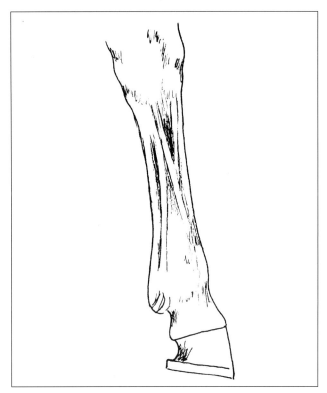

Illus. 10-5. **Prominent tendons on a lower leg.**

Starting Points

Once again, a good place to start carving is to round off any areas that you have left sharp or too square when roughing out. After the leg is closer to its final shape, a next logical step is to start carving the lower legs, since they are all basically the same.

Carving the Cannon, Fetlock, Pastern, Coronet, and Hoof

The least-intimidating place to begin carving lower-leg detail is on the hoof. Using a V-parting tool, outline the groove between the coronet and the hoof, and the groove between the horseshoe (if you are carving horseshoes) and the hoof. The coronet overhangs the hoof, and the horseshoe can stick out very slightly from the hoof, so use a medium gouge with a shallow sweep to shave down the hoof a bit between the two. The coronet should protrude more than the horseshoe. When carving the hoof, be careful to keep the front angle of the hoof the same as it was before you started carving.

Using a medium gouge with a shallow sweep, round off the edge of the coronet so that it resem-

bles a slight roll around the hoof. (Remember to round from a high point, which, in this case, would be a little above the bottom edge of the coronet.)

If you look at an anatomy book and the Carving Gallery at the end of this chapter, you will see that the coronet angles down on each side as it circles the back of the hoof. It ends in a soft-pointed V at the back of the hoof. Carve the back of the coronet to match the examples.

In an anatomy book, you'll see that just above the coronet in the back, there is a recessed area that resembles a triangle which points down and has a broad U-shaped top. Draw this area; then use a medium gouge with a medium sweep to carve out the recess.

Next, move to the pastern area. From the high point of the front of the coronet, the pastern area has a slight dip and then makes a gentle curve up the front of the leg. This characteristic should be correct on your animal's leg without any carving (remember the centerline). If you look at the pastern on a drawing of a horse from the front, you'll note that the sides curve in and out. Using a medium gouge with a shallow sweep, shape the sides of the pastern. Next, smooth out the back side of the pastern, below the fetlock, tapering it in from the curved sides.

The fetlock, as we mentioned above, is somewhat like a ball. Draw a small circle about a quarter-size on each side of the fetlock to use as a high point. Then use a medium gouge with a shallow sweep to carve out from each circle to round the fetlock sides. The back of the fetlock has a knobby bone that protrudes, with a small tuft of hair descending from the bone. On most carousel horses, just the bone sticks out, and the tuft is omitted. Using a medium gouge with a shallow sweep, round the bone. Leave a little wood protruding down, if you want to include the tuft.

Look at Illus. 10-2 and the Carving Gallery again and note that the cannon tapers in from the fetlock, and then flares out again as it approaches the knee. Using a large gouge with a shallow sweep, carve the gentle curves of the cannon.

On the back of the cannon, there is a prominent tendon that runs up into the upper leg. Draw the lines defining the tendon, which will be the high point on the back of the leg. Using a medium gouge with a medium sweep, carve shallow grooves on each side of the tendon, so the tendon sticks out. Then use a shallow-sweep gouge to smooth the transition between the outer edge of the grooves and the curve of the side of the cannon.

Next, look at Illus. 10-5 and the Carving Gallery again to note the tendons on the sides of the cannon. Using a medium gouge with a deep sweep, carve away only enough wood just outside the lines defining the tendons so that the tendons stand up slightly in relief. Using the center of the tendon as the high point, round over each one so they are raised and rounded, rather than raised and flat.

Carving the Knees on the Front Legs

As we said earlier, the knees are somewhat rounded like balls, with slightly flat sides. On the sides, the two bones that come together are visible, as is the shallow groove between them. To carve the front knees, first look at the photographs of the knee area in the Carving Gallery and an animal-anatomy book. Draw two circles on each side of the knee, one on top of the other with a small space in between, to outline the bones. Since the bones are kind of knobby, draw a small circle inside each of the other circles to represent the high point (the knob) of the bone area.

Using a small veiner, carve out a shallow groove between the two large circles on each side of the knee. Then use a medium gouge with a shallow sweep to carve out from the small circles to round the two bones. Smooth out the transition from the bones to the groove.

The front of the knee area is a relatively flat continuation of the line from the cannon to the upper leg. Because of the centerline, the front of the knee (at the high point) should be accurate without any carving.

Using a medium gouge with a shallow sweep, round the front of the knee where necessary so it blends smoothly into the sides. Round the back of the knee to complete the ball-like effect. Note, however, that the tendon that runs up the back of the leg starts to be more prominent again as the top of the knee blends into the upper leg. Shape the back of the knee accordingly.

If your horse has a front knee that is bent, note that the knee takes on a somewhat different shape, as shown in Illus. 10-4. The two bones are still prominent and still have the groove between them, but the top of the knee flattens out. Look at

your photograph or pattern for guidance.

Carving the Knees on the Hind Legs

The knees on the hind legs are much like the knees on the front legs, with a few added elements. The sides of the knees have the same two bones that show, with the shallow groove between them, and the front of the knee continues the smooth line from the cannon to the upper leg (though at a different angle). Consequently, you can use the directions for the front knees to carve these areas.

However, if you look at an anatomy book and the full-view photos in the Carving Gallery, you'll see that on the back of the knee, just above where the two bones come together, there is a bone that sticks out (called the hock), covered by a large tendon running up the back of the leg. This bone gives the back of the leg a kind of point.

To carve this area, use an anatomy book and your photograph or pattern to determine where to draw a small circle outlining the narrow round knob of the protruding bone. Then draw lines defining the large tendon as it leaves the knob and runs up the back of the leg. Using a medium gouge with a medium sweep, carve away the wood around the bottom and sides of the circle, so that the knob stands out very prominently. Then carve a prominent groove on each side of the tendon as it starts to go up the back of the leg, and smooth out the transition from the outside of the grooves to the sides of the legs.

Carving the Upper Legs

As mentioned earlier, at Horsin' Around we recommend that carvers wait to carve the details of the upper legs until the horse is assembled, so that a smooth transition can be carved where the upper leg joins the body. Directions for carving this area are provided in Chapter 12.

Carving the "Frog"

If your horse has a leg that is raised and bent, you might want to carve the bottom of the horseshoe and the "frog" (a V-shaped wedge on the bottom of the hoof) to make your horse look more realistic. Look at the Carving Gallery and an animal-anatomy book, and draw the lines designating the bottom of the horseshoe.

Using a medium gouge with a shallow sweep,

carve out a thin layer of wood inside the horse-shoe so the shoe stands up in relief. Next, draw the lines of the V-shaped frog, and outline them with the V-parting tool. Using the shallow-sweep gouge, dig out the depression inside the V, using the photographs in the Carving Gallery and the anatomy book as a guide.

Do not carve the bottom of any of the hoofs that will be standing on the base. Leaving them flat will give your horse more surface area to stand on and help make it more stable.

CARVING TECHNIQUES FOR MENAGERIE ANIMAL CARVERS

All the carving instructions presented above can apply to menagerie animals. The key to carving your animal successfully is knowing what it looks like in three dimensions. Look at an anatomy book and a three-dimensional model to determine over-all leg shape. Then look at photographs of real animals to see what bone and muscle structure actually shows. Draw on the prominent details, determining what are "high" areas and what are "low"

areas. Work on getting the overall shape of the legs right, before you start refining the details.

COMMON CARVING MISTAKES

Here are some common mistakes to avoid when carving the legs:

1. Don't carve a lot of leg detail if the rest of your animal is not done in a realistic style.

2. Don't carve legs that don't match each other. They should be similar in both detail and proportion.

3. Don't overcarve the legs so that they are too spindly for the animal.

CARVING GALLERY

Illus. 10-6 to 10-12 are photographs of carving techniques and close-ups of different features on the legs of carousel animals that you can refer to when carving. *The Carving Gallery photos were taken by Thomas L. Cory.*

Illus. 10-6. After the leg blank is glued up, the leg's front profile should be drawn on the wood to aid in roughing out.

Illus. 10-7. Using an angle grinder to remove excess wood is a fast way of roughing out the leg.

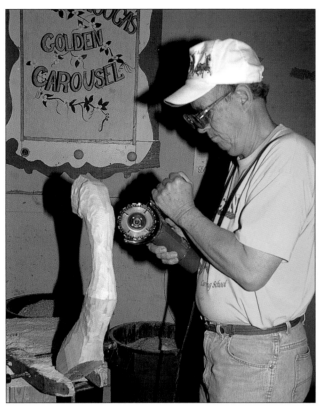

Illus. 10-8. Someone who is experienced with an angle grinder can rough out a leg very close to its finished shape.

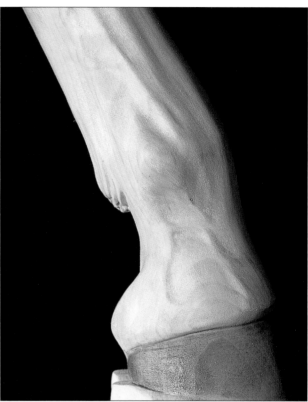

Illus. 10-9. This carefully carved leg clearly shows the fetlock, pastern, coronet, and hoof.

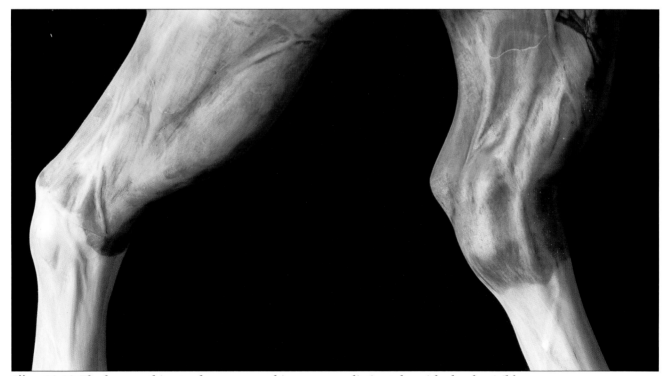

Illus. 10-10. The legs on this stander are carved in a very realistic style, with clearly visible bones, muscle, and veins.

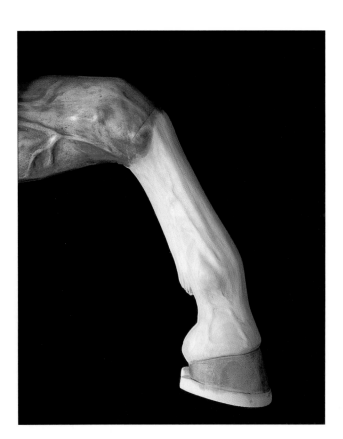

Illus. 10-11. The different parts of this leg have been carved in good proportion to each other and the rest of the leg.

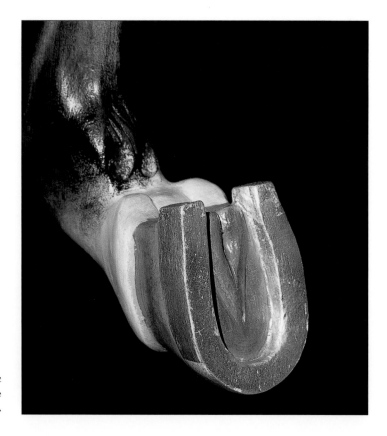

Illus. 10-12. A raised leg looks much more realistic if the "frog" (a V-shaped wedge on the bottom of the hoof) and the underside of the horseshoe are carved.

11

Preparing and Carving the Body

At first glance, building and carving the body of your carousel animal can appear to be a daunting task. It's big, it's heavy, and it involves carving a lot of wood. But remember that you build and carve the body just like you build and carve all the other parts of the animal: step-by-step.

Many people don't realize that the bodies of the antique carousel animals were hollow. They were built using "coffin"-style construction, so named because the glued-up body frame looks somewhat like a coffin (Illus. 11-1). We use this same method at Horsin' Around, because it saves not only wood but weight. The coffin-style construction body is still heavy, but not nearly as heavy as a solid-wood body.

The techniques you used to carve the head, mane, and tail will also be used to carve the body. One difference is that the body often involves some very fine detail carving. Saddles and trappings often have finely carved grooves and decorative edges. Sometimes figures—such as angels, birds, monkeys, and dogs—are carved hanging off the romance side or on the saddle back (cantle).

If your animal is finely detailed, you might want to consider purchasing the micro-carving tools we described in Chapter 2, if you haven't already. They can be purchased from woodworking stores and catalogs, and are very useful when you're carving very small details.

The body should be heavy enough that you don't have to keep it secured at all times when you are carving it; but when you need to position it on its side or upside down, you'll have to figure out how to keep it from moving so you don't injure yourself or make a bad cut. At Horsin' Around, we build a rectangular frame which is wider and shorter than the animal, and then cut big notches in the end boards to cradle the body. We then cover the edges of the frame with carpet so they don't dent the wood, as shown in Illus. 11-5 in the Carving Gallery section. If you are securing the body to a small table, you might be able to use large band clamps. One other way to secure the body, which is considerably less stable, is to prop it with strategically placed wedges of scrap wood.

MAKING THE CARVING BLANK

The first thing you have to do is cut out the body pattern from the blueprint to make the body side panels. Since the body pattern is large, line up two or three planks of wood (depending on the size of your animal), spread the pattern out over the planks, and then trace the pattern onto the wood. Repeat the process to trace the pieces for the second side panel.

Next, cut out each piece using the band saw. Mark the pieces as you cut them out, such as "romance side top" and "romance side middle," so you don't get the pieces mixed up. Then sand the edges a bit to get rid of any splintered areas that might interfere with gluing.

Next, line up the pieces of one of the panels, coat the adjoining surfaces with glue, and glue the pieces together to make the full panel. After about 5 minutes, clamp the pieces together with a large pipe clamp. Repeat this process for the other side panel. Let the pieces dry for several hours—longer if the weather is especially cold or humid.

To make the "coffin" body, begin by measuring the widest point of your side panels from breast to rump. Then cut out two boards as described below:

Large animal: Cut two 2-inch boards $9\frac{1}{2}$ inches wide by the panel length.

Medium animal: Cut two 2-inch boards $8\frac{1}{2}$ inches wide by the panel length.

Small animal: Cut two 2-inch boards $7\frac{3}{4}$-8 inches wide by the panel length.

Coat both gluing surfaces with glue, and glue the two boards one on top of the other to form the base of the body, as shown in Illus. 11-1. Next, cut a series of smaller boards to stack on the base along the front and back of the body. It is important that you cut the small boards across the grain, so that you don't have end grain on the breast and rump, since end grain is difficult to carve. The

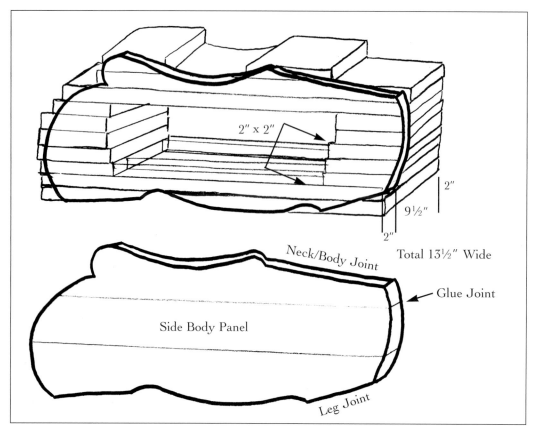

2" x 2"

2"

9½"

2"

Neck/Body Joint

Total 13½" Wide

Glue Joint

Side Body Panel

Leg Joint

Illus. 11-1. **Coffin-style construction. Follow these guidelines: 1. Be sure to glue both surfaces. 2. Signing and dating the inside of the body is a nice touch. 3. Always put 2 x 2's in the four inside corners.**

length of the small boards should be the same as the width of the body base (e.g., 9½ inches for a large animal). The width can vary as needed to accommodate the curves of your end panel, as long as the boards aren't any narrower than about 8 inches or so.

How many smaller boards you need obviously varies with the height of the body. As shown in Illus. 11-1, you need to leave enough room on the top of the body to stack another two full-length boards, to complete the "coffin" top. These two 2-inch boards should be cut the width of your base and the length of the body panel at that point of the body. Finally, add two smaller boards to the top of the body to provide enough wood for the high points of the saddle.

Once you have all the pieces cut and fitted, glue them together piece by piece, making sure to thoroughly coat each gluing surface. To make the body stronger, cut one 2 x 2 to fit into each of the four inside corners, and glue them into the corners as shown.

Once the body frame is completely glued together, wait 5 minutes. Then clamp the frame by using pipe clamps. Let it dry for several hours-longer if it's especially cold or humid.

At this point, many carvers like to sign and date the inside of the body. Most of the master carvers at the turn of the century did not sign their carvings in any way, so historians today can only guess who carved some of the animals, based on the style. We encourage our carvers at Horsin' Around to sign theirs, so that years from now people will know who carved the animal and when. Instead of signing the inside, some carvers carve their initials in an unobtrusive place, such as on the strap on the underside of the belly.

When the body frame is dry, remove the clamps so you can attach the side panels. Before attaching the panels, use a hand-held planer or a belt sander to even up the edges of the small boards, so the panels have level surfaces to be glued to.

Next, lay the side panels one on top of the

other, and align them so they match perfectly. Then draw one line (perpendicular) across the chest edges of the panels, one line across the top edges, and one line across the rump edges. These lines will help you align the panels when you glue them to the body frame. Not having them aligned perfectly when they are glued on the body frame will cause carving problems later on.

Next, place one panel on a table, its outside surface down. Then turn the body frame on its side and place it on top of the panel, lining it up appropriately. Trace around the inside and outside of the frame on the panel, so you will know where to put glue on the panel. Then place the other panel on a table, outside surface down, and repeat the process.

Apply glue to the edges of the body frame and the area inside the lines that you just traced on the panels. Glue the side panels to the body, with the body on its side. Wait five minutes, and then use a yardstick to make sure that the alignment lines on one panel match up with the alignment lines on the other panel.

Now, either tap in small finishing nails at an angle to keep the boards from sliding around, or clamp the frame using cinch straps, pipe clamps, or C-clamps. Let the blank dry for several hours—longer if it's especially cold or humid.

If your animal's body does not have any detail on it that sticks out significantly on the romance side, then the body blank should be thick enough at this point for you to carve everything you need out of it without adding on any extra wood. If your animal has something like a bird or cherub on its side, however, you might need to add on a 1- or 2-inch-thick chunk of board on the romance side where the element is, to provide enough wood to carve it. Use your photograph or pattern and the blueprint for guidance.

Bear in mind, however, that most figures and side elements on the original carousel animals don't protrude very far, because little legs have to be able to straddle the animal without getting poked. Look at the photographs in the Carving Gallery at the end of this chapter to see some good examples. Also, if your animal has a delicate element such as roses or bells, you might want to carve those separately and peg them onto the body, rather than add additional wood to the body.

Roughing Out the Body

When the body blank is dry, remove the finishing nails or clamps. Then use a large, shallow-sweep gouge and mallet (or an angle grinder with a chain-saw blade) to carve away the wood on the breast and rump that sticks out beyond the profile of the side panels. Don't take off any wood from the side panels themselves, except where you need to round a square edge, since the side view of the animal is accurate at this point.

Be very careful to shape the flat area where the neck attaches to the body so that it is a level surface (Illus. 11-2). One way to do this is to carve out the wood and then even out the surface with a hand-held planer and/or a belt sander. Use the same care and methods in shaping the flat surfaces where the legs attach to the body.

Next, you can take off the wood on the bottom of the body that sticks out below the profile of the side panels. When you're done, you should have a body blank that matches the shape of the side panels. You can also rough out the depression on the rump at this time, as shown in Illus. 11-2.

Carving Techniques for Menagerie Animal Carvers If you are carving a menagerie animal instead of a horse, follow the same instructions above for cutting out and gluing up the body side panels and building the "coffin" body. You will also rough out the animal the same way. You can do additional roughing out if your animal doesn't have a saddle or trappings on the body (such as a bare zebra). Look at an animal-anatomy book (or a three-dimensional model) to get the general shape, sketch on the shape from all views, and then use a large, shallow-sweep gouge and a mallet to carve away the excess wood outside the lines.

PEGGING THE NECK AND LEGS TO THE BODY

Before starting to carve body detail, it's a good idea to peg the neck and legs to the body so you don't inadvertently carve away any wood that is needed at the joint areas. Once again, we use 3/4-inch hardwood dowel for pegs, a 3/4-inch spade bit, and 3/4-inch metal dowel centers.

Pegging the Neck

First, position the head/neck on the flat base area where the neck meets the body. When you have the neck where you want it, trace around the outside of it to mark where the neck will be on the body.

Next, make sure the body is secure. Then drill two 2-inch-deep holes in the neck base on the body, each one about 2 inches in from the top and bottom ends of the base; be careful to ensure that each hole is perpendicular to the plane of the base. Place the metal dowel centers in the holes.

Now, reposition the neck on the body, using the traced outline to accurately line up the two pieces. Using a mallet, tap the head/neck onto the body so that the points of the dowel centers make a physical impression in the base of the neck, indicating where you must drill the corresponding holes.

Next, remove the head/neck from the body. Clamp the head/neck to the worktable, neck base up, and (using the marks from the metal dowel centers) drill the two corresponding 2-inch holes into the base of the neck, again being careful to ensure that the holes are perpendicular to the plane of the base.

Now, cut two 3¾-inch lengths of dowel, and mark them so you know they are for the head. You don't want to glue the head/neck to the body at this time, but it's a good idea to put the pegs in the holes and test the neck/body joint, in case you need to make any modifications to the wood or the dowels to get a good fit.

Do your best to get the surfaces flat so the fit is close, but don't spend hours trying to make it perfect. If it's not perfect, you can insert thin wood wedges into the joint to fix problem areas when you assemble and glue the body.

Pegging the Legs

To peg the legs to the body, turn the body upside down, supporting it in a wooden cradle (as discussed in the beginning of this chapter) or propping it upright with a few strategically placed wedges of wood. Position the leg on the flat base area where the leg meets the body. When you have the leg where you want it, trace around its outside to mark its position on the body.

Next, make sure the body is secured. Then drill two 2-inch-deep holes in the leg base on the body, each one about 2 inches in from the top and bottom ends of the traced leg outline, being careful to ensure that each hole is perpendicular to the plane of the base. Place the metal dowel centers in the holes.

Now, reposition the leg on the body, using the traced outline to accurately line up the two pieces. Using a mallet, tap the leg onto the body, so that the points of the dowel centers make a physical impression in the base of the leg, indicating where you must drill the corresponding holes. Remove the leg from the body, clamp it to the worktable, leg base up, and (using the marks from the metal dowel centers) drill the two corresponding 2-inch holes in the base of the leg, again being careful to ensure the holes are perpendicular to the plane of the base. Repeat the entire process for each leg.

Cut two 3¾-inch lengths of dowel for each leg, and mark them so you know which dowels go with which leg. As with the head/neck, you don't want to glue the legs to the body at this time, but it's a good idea to put the pegs in the holes and test the leg/body joints, in case you need to make any modifications to the wood or the dowels to get a good fit.

DRAWING PROMINENT FEATURES AND TRAPPINGS

Turn the body on its left side, and place the body pattern on the romance side panel. Slip some carbon paper (ink side towards the wood) between your pattern and the panel. Then retrace the detail lines of your pattern to transfer the markings to the wood. Unless you have really large carbon paper, you'll have to move the paper around as you work. It will help to tape the pattern down in a few places to keep it from shifting.

Before tracing the markings onto the left side of the animal, take time to modify your pattern. On American carousels, the left side of the animal was not normally as ornate as the romance side—as shown in the Carving Gallery. Some decorative elements were carried over to the left side, but most major decorations were carved only on the romance side since that was the side spectators saw.

Look at your pattern and decide which elements you need to have on both sides (such as the saddle, blanket, straps, and whatever decorations you want to repeat) and which elements you want to omit from the left side. Using a different-colored pencil or marker from your original markings, remark the lines that you plan to transfer to the left side. If your animal has something large covering the saddle on the romance side—such as an eagle clutching a partially unfurled flag—you might not

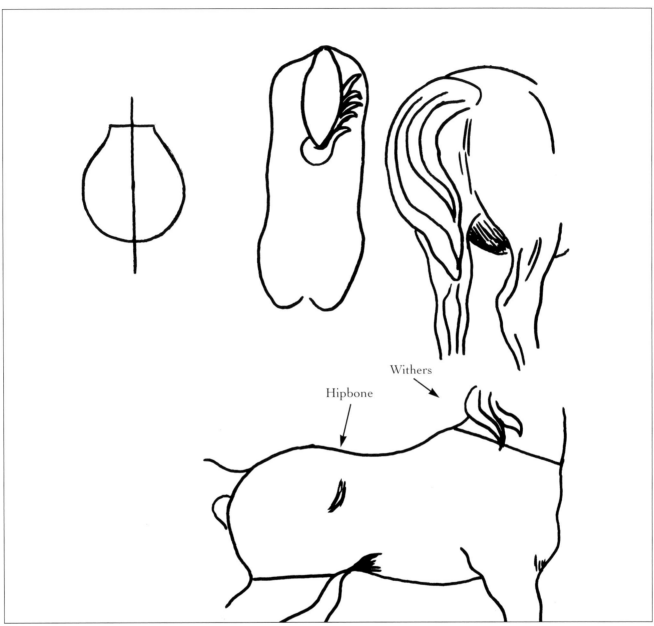

Illus. 11-2. **Guide for roughing out the body for a carousel horse.**

be able to see how long the saddle is, or even what shape it is on the bottom. If that's the case, look at photographs of other carousel animals, or maybe real saddles, and decide what you want the saddle to look like. Then sketch the shape on your pattern so that it can be carved on the left side, where it will show. Use the same process to draw any other elements missing from your pattern.

When your pattern has been modified, turn the body over, place the flipped pattern and the carbon paper on the left side, and retrace the remarked/redrawn detail lines of your pattern to transfer the markings to the wood. (If you can't see the lines of your pattern through the paper when you flip it over, tape it up on a window and trace the lines onto the back side of the pattern.)

When you have transferred all the lines, draw in any connecting lines you might have skipped when modifying the pattern, as well as any straps that wrap around the body. When you are finished, you should have a body blank with all the details drawn on it.

Finally, looking at Illus. 11-2, draw in the hipbone. It may not be visible on the romance side (though often it is), but it should probably be visible on the left side (except, for example, on an armored horse). Then, if you're carving a realistic-style horse, use Illus. 11-3 to draw the muscles on the chest.

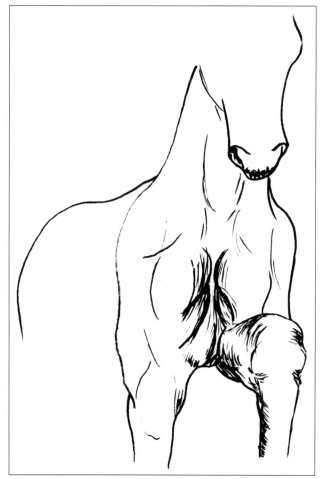

Illus. 11-3. **Neck and chest muscles.**

As with the head, ideally all the lines you transferred to the body blank should match the pattern—and thus the original animal—exactly. Since you are working with a lumpy piece of wood, however, lines that should be straight probably didn't transfer exactly straight, and round circles probably didn't transfer exactly round, etc. At this point, it's a good idea to look at the markings on the wood and correct or redraw ones that you think will be a problem. Once again, use a clear, flexible acrylic ruler to straighten lines that should be relatively straight, such as those on the straps. As with the head, correcting these small details so that they can be carved more accurately will enhance the quality of your carving.

Now, spend a few moments looking at the body blank, a photograph or pattern of your animal, and an anatomical drawing of your animal, noting how they all correspond. Just as you did with the head, stop looking at the body as a whole, and start visualizing it as a group of lines, curves, and three-dimensional layers. Look at each detail, and note how it relates to other details. Once you feel reasonably familiar with how the body blank now looks and how it should look when you're done, you're ready to start carving.

FINDING THE ANIMAL IN THE WOOD

Every animal is so different that it's difficult to give specific directions on how to carve the body. The photograph or pattern of your animal is your best guide, as well as the photographs in the Carving Gallery. Looking at photographs of real-life objects (or the objects themselves, when possible) can also be very helpful. For example, if you are trying to carve the feathers on an eagle, find a good close-up photograph, or even a nature coloring book, to see what kind of feathers they show. Remember that while you can carve exact replicas of an element, it's not really necessary. The most important thing is to carve something in such a way that it *suggests* the real item.

Before you start to carve, draw the centerline on the top of the body. Don't carve across that line unless it's unavoidable.

Basically, the best approach you can take to carving the body is to decide which elements stick out the most (what is high), outline them with a V-parting tool, and then reduce the wood around them a bit until you get to the level of the second layer of elements. Then repeat the process with the second layer of elements, the third layer, etc. It's the same approach you used to carve the head; the body just has more layers of elements and detail to deal with.

As with the other parts of the horse, you don't want to carve one area of the body completely and then move to another area. Instead, you want to carve a little everywhere, and then keep moving around to reduce the wood little by little all over the body until it starts to take the shape you want. The detail lines you drew on the wood are your best guide, so keep redrawing them when you have to carve them off until you don't need them anymore.

Starting Points

A good place to start is to define the major decorations and side figures, since they often protrude the most from your animal and thus are your highest carving points. If you're carving a figure, look at the photograph of your animal to see how three-dimensional your figure actually should be.

On the antique carousel animals, some figures are relief carvings and some are more like sculpture partially carved into the animal's side or on the saddle. The figures that are sculpted are not a full three-dimensional version of the figure, however. They are carved so they have the illusion of being three-dimensional, but in actuality fade into the animal. Look at the photographs in the Carving Gallery to see several versions of side and saddle figures.

Carving the Decorations and Side Figures

Look at the decorations and/or figures, and determine which is high and which is low. Shade the high areas, and mark the lower areas with X's. Then outline the elements with a V-parting tool, and remove a little wood around the element until you reach the level of the next layer. Outline the next layer, remove a little wood around the element, and so on.

If you're carving a figure, look at it as a series of lines and curves, and replicate them in the wood. The photograph or pattern of your animal is your best guide. Be careful to round elements when they are supposed to be rounded, and avoid fooling yourself into thinking you're making the figure three-dimensional by making the different parts of the figure all the same level with grooves in between.

If your animal has elements such as tassels or ribbons, think about what they look like in real life and try to replicate them on the wood. If a ribbon is folded, carve it in different level layers so it resembles a real ribbon.

Carving the Saddle, Blanket, and Trappings

Remember that the centerline going down the saddle gives you the correct profile of the horse without the need for any carving. Don't carve across that line, or the profile of your horse will not look right. Begin by using the V-parting tool to outline the lines of the saddle. Then use a gouge to reduce the wood to the next layer of elements, which will probably include the straps. The blanket will probably be at the third layer, depending on your animal.

The raised center in the front of the saddle is called the pommel. At the pommel, the base of the neck and the back of the shoulders both narrow to meet and form the withers, which is a narrow, rounded area. To shape the pommel, you will first have to remove some wood at the back of the neck on each side, and then shape the withers. Don't carve into the traced outline of the neck, however, or it will be a problem when you assemble the animal.

The width of the saddle is very rounded. Use a large, shallow-sweep gouge to round it off, taking care to make the curve smooth and natural and to make the two sides balanced. Keep in mind as you carve that the curves of the original carousel saddles were comfortable for kids to straddle. If the saddle blanket on your animal has folds or wrinkles in it, carve it in different layers just as a real blanket would fold.

Flowers

Flowers look difficult to carve, but you actually just carve them in layers like other elements. If your flower is flat like a daisy, outline the shape with the V-parting tool, and then carve away wood to leave the flower in relief. Finally, angle the petals so they are high at their outer edges and descend as they approach the middle of the flower.

If your animal has a rose on it, carve it separately, and then peg it onto the animal. First, cut a small square of wood a bit bigger than your finished rose will be, and glue it to another wood chunk, so that it can be clamped in a vise, as shown in Illus. 11-4. Draw on the rose shape and then rough it out. Start the detail carving at the outside, and work in. Shape the outer petals; then cut away to the next layer and shape them, etc.

Carving Muscle and Bone Definition

There are several anatomical features of the body that you need to carve to make the horse look realistic. One of the most important is the hips, which are the widest part of the body. On real horses, the hips are squarish-looking. Draw the hipbone on the horse, as shown in Illus. 11-2. Use a large gouge with a shallow sweep to lower the area in front of the hip a bit, so the hip stands high. The hip very gradually tapers rearward, until it starts to curve around the rump. Don't forget to carve the hipbone on both sides of the horse.

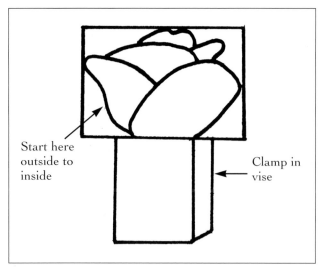

Start here outside to inside

Clamp in vise

Illus. 11-4. **Carving a rose peg on a body.**

The chest area also has some muscle definition which you might want to carve if your animal is realistic in style. Look at Illus. 11-3 and the Carving Gallery again to get a feel for what the chest looks like. When you carve the muscles, carve them so they are rounded, rather than in sharp relief. If you look at an anatomy book, you'll see that the shoulders also have some prominent muscles. As with the chest muscles, carve them so they are rounded.

You also need to carve the underside of the body. Your best bet here is to look at a good plastic model or realistic toy and shape your animal to match. Don't carve too much on the underside until you assemble your animal, however, since it involves some transition areas.

Setting Jewels

Some of the antique animals were decorated with faux jewels. If you want to add jewels to your ani-

mal, first place the jewel on the wood and trace around it. Next, cut or drill a 1/4-inch-deep hole inside the traced area. Before adding the jewel, apply gold leaf to its back. Then squirt a little glue in the hole, and press in the jewel.

CARVING INSTRUCTIONS FOR MENAGERIE ANIMAL CARVERS

All the carving instructions presented above apply to menagerie animals. Once again, the key to carving your animal successfully is knowing what it looks like in three dimensions. Familiarize yourself with the anatomy of your animal's body before you begin to carve.

COMMON CARVING MISTAKES

. Here are some common mistakes to avoid when carving the body:

1. Don't leave the area at the withers too fat.

2. Don't leave the body too square. It should be rounded.

3. When carving figures on the side of the body, don't carve a recessed area around the figures. The figures should rise out of the body surface.

CARVING GALLERY

Illus. 11-5 to 11-23 show carving techniques and close-ups of different carved features of the body, saddle, and trappings that you can refer to when carving. *The Carving Gallery photographs were taken by Thomas L. Cory.*

Illus. 11-5. Turning the horse upside down in some sort of cradle (this one made of scrap wood and carpet chunks) makes it easier to carve and sand the underside.

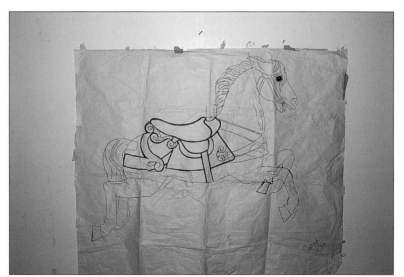

Illus. 11-6. It's helpful when carving the body to have your blueprint tacked up where you can refer to it often.

Illus. 11-7. It's a good idea when laminating a blank to cut out all the pieces before gluing the layers together.

Illus. 11-8. A laminated blank.

Illus. 11-9 and *11-10.* Though many horses have more ornate trappings on the romance side than on the left side, this horse (with the romance side shown here and the left side shown below) has been carved to be the same on both sides.

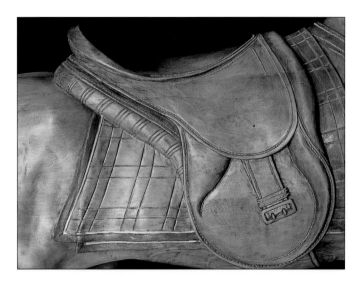

Illus. 11-11. The fine detail carved into this saddle and blanket make it look as if they are real.

Illus. 11-12. The simulated stitching on this saddle is done by carving a narrow groove where the stitching will go, punching small holes in an evenly spaced pattern, stretching the string over the groove, poking the string into the holes, and putting a little glue into each hole.

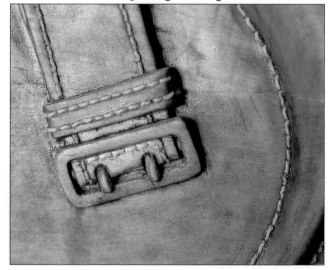

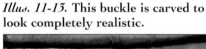

Illus. 11-13. This buckle is carved to look completely realistic.

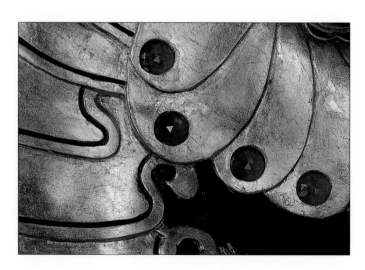

Illus. 11-14. This armor is carved in overlapping layers, to look like real armor.

Illus. 11-15. This hunting horse's saddle is adorned with a rifle and an unlucky rabbit.

Illus. 11-16. Elements such as this rifle are carved to be only partially raised from the surface, since elements that protrude too far from the horse would hurt the legs of the person riding the animal.

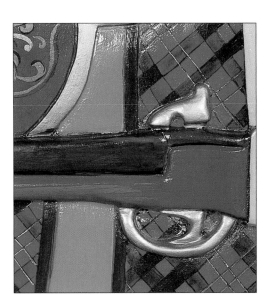

Illus. 11-17. This Indian pony has a beautifully carved fox as a saddle.

Illus. 11-18. The steps involved in carving elements such as these grapes include drawing the shape on the wood, deciding what's high and low, and starting to carve the layers.

Illus. 11-19. The best way to learn how to carve elements such as bells is to look at an example of the real thing, concentrating on its shape and layers.

Illus. 11-20. The eagle on this horse is carved in relief rather than completely three-dimensional.

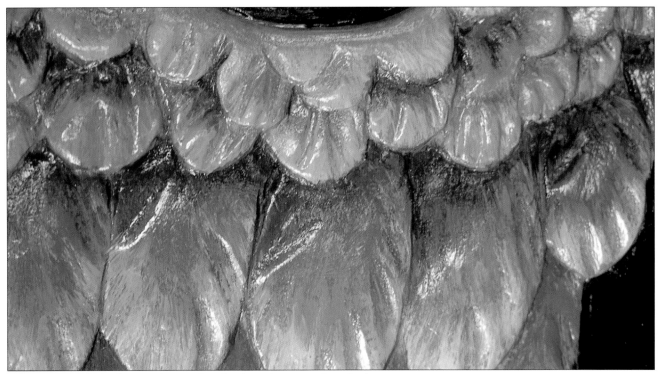

Illus. 11-21. A key element in carving feathers is to overlap the layers.

Illus. 11-22. Three-dimensional elements such as these bells can be carved separately, and then pegged and glued onto the side of the animal.

Illus. 11-23. Some carvers like to name their animals, and carve the name somewhere on the animal's saddle or trappings.

12

Assembling Your Animal

You now have a pile of carved horse pieces at your feet, and you're probably anxious to put them together to make your animal. Assembly is relatively simple. The most important thing to remember is that anything that doesn't fit quite right can be fixed.

You should have already pegged and fit the head and legs to the body in Chapter 11. The only piece left to install is the tail.

INSTALLING THE TAIL

When you carved the tail in Chapter 9, you modified your pattern to add a 4-inch extension to insert into the body. Look at your photograph or pattern and the photographs in the Carving Gallery in Chapter 9 to determine where to place the tail.

When you have determined the position, hold the tail extension up to the body and trace the shape of the extension onto the body. Using a drill with a large bit, drill out the center of the 4-inch hole to remove as much wood within the traced area as possible. Then use a flat chisel to carve out the rest of the hole to match the shape and depth of the extension.

Next, check that the tail extension fits well in the hole. Then coat the extension and the inside of the hole with glue, and glue in the tail. Let the tail dry several hours-longer if it is especially cold or humid.

To make the tail joint stronger and lessen the chance of its breaking off, you have to peg it to both the rump and a leg (if possible). First, drill a 1/2-inch hole from the top of the rump down into the extension (we usually drill 6 inches down), perpendicular to the extension, as shown in Illus. 9-1 in Chapter 9. Then place a little glue in the hole, and insert a 1/2-inch dowel coated with glue through the hole and into the tail extension. Carve or saw off the end of the dowel flush with the surface. If the tail passes close to a leg, drill a hole through the tail and into the leg, and then peg the tail to the leg. The size of the dowel peg will depend on the size of the tail at the peg location.

Chapter 9 provides instructions for installing a real horsehair tail. If you're using a real tail, installing it should be the very last step of your project, after all the decorative painting and the final clear coats are done.

CARVING THE TRANSITION AREAS

Now it's time to put the pieces together so you can carve the transition areas. Look at the photograph or pattern of your animal, an animal-anatomy book, a three-dimensional plastic model, and the photos in the Carving Galleries to see what the transition areas of the neck and legs look like. Draw the appropriate lines to define the areas.

Neck Transition Areas

There is a major definition line where the neck meets the body. Continue the smooth neck muscles downward until they run into the shoulders. The shoulders then curve forward around the bottom of the front of the neck, where they blend into the chest.

Upper-Leg Transition Areas

At this point, you need to assess how well each leg is sized in proportion to the body. Carve a little more on the legs if they're too fat, being careful to keep them in proportion to each other as well as the body.

The upper legs have a prominent muscle or two that you can define if you are carving a realistic horse. Look at Illus. 10-4 and the photos in the Chapter 10 Carving Gallery, and draw the lines on your wood to match. Look at your photograph or pattern and an animal-anatomy book to see how the upper-leg muscles blend into the body, and then carve them accordingly. Once again, the muscles should be subtle and rounded, rather than sharp.

Underside of Horse

As mentioned in Chapter 11, your best bet for carving the underside of the horse is to look at a small plastic model and shape your animal to match. Basically, a horse's belly is rounded. The insides of the upper legs (where you added on the extra wood) have a V-shaped muscle that has to be rounded and blended into the legs. There is a depression between the legs.

UNDERCUTTING

One thing you can do to significantly improve the look of your carving is to undercut such things as the saddle and straps, to make them look as if they are placed on top the animal (as in real life). To do this, use a V-parting tool to carefully cut away a little wood under each edge.

EVENING UP THE LEGS

If your animal is a stander, before you glue up the body pieces you have to make sure the legs are even, so that the animal can stand with all the required hoofs flat on the platform or floor. At Horsin' Around, we made what we call a "leg board" to help us determine whether the legs are even or not. The board is 60 inches long and 8 inches wide.

To use the leg board, we turn the animal body upside down in a wooden cradle, insert the legs, and then place the board on top of the hoofs to simulate the hoofs standing on the floor. If a hoof does not "stand" flat on the board, we insert thin wedges or shims of wood into the joint where the leg meets the body, to correct the position of the leg. The shims are glued in when we glue up all the pieces.

Even if you corrected the horse's stance in your pattern, it might still have a leg that is too short. If that's the case, you can correct the leg's length by tracing the shape of the end of the upper leg onto a thin piece of wood, cutting it out, and gluing it on top of the leg (where it meets the body) to make the leg longer. If you do this, you'll obviously have to drill your peg holes through the new wood and modify the length of the leg pegs.

There is one other thing you need to check on the legs: whether they are facing in the right direction. Sight down the side of the horse and make sure the hoofs are all facing directly forward. You don't want your animal to look pigeon-toed or bow-legged.

GLUING THE BODY TOGETHER

When you feel that the pieces fit together well, the legs are even, and you've carved the transition areas, it's time to glue up the pieces. For each two pieces to be glued together, put a little glue into each dowel hole, insert the dowel, coat both gluing surfaces with glue, and put the pieces together. After about five minutes, clamp the pieces together using any clamps you can get to work. Let the assembly dry for several hours—longer if it's especially cold or humid.

INSERTING THE POLE

At this point, you need to decide whether you want to insert a pole through your animal. If you carved a jumper, you have no choice; it has to have the pole to hold it up. If you carved a stander, you have several choices. Some carvers choose to omit the pole, and instead mount the animal onto a base, inserting screws up through the base into the hoofs to help keep the horse stable. Others choose to use a partial pole, which runs from the base up to the underside of the horse, but does not go through the animal. Many carvers go the classic route, inserting a standard carousel pole through the animal to make it look like it just came off a carousel. Both partial and full-size poles can be ordered from supply houses. Most people prefer to use brass poles.

If you're going to use a standard carousel pole, you need to order one with a 1-inch outside diameter (1/2-inch inside diameter) for a stander, and a 2-inch outside diameter (1¼-inch inside diameter) for a jumper. The jumper needs a stronger pole since the pole is the only thing that is holding it up.

To install a classic pole through the animal, you will need a spade bit the same size as the outside diameter of the pole and at least 6 inches long. First, mark where you are going to put the hole. It should be just in front of the pommel (center front of the saddle) and centered side-to-side. Next, drill a hole straight down from the top about 6 inches deep (or at least deep enough to hit the body cavity). When you look into the hole, you should be able to see into the body cavity.

Now, stand up a yardstick on the side of the body, directly lined up vertically with the hole, and mark on the bottom of the animal's side where the hole would be if it were extended. Carefully extend the line under the body until it's at a point that is centered from side-to-side on the body.

Double-check the markings, because it's critical that the holes line up, both side-to-side and front-to-back, or the pole will be tilted. Then turn the animal over and drill a 6-inch hole straight down into the belly of the body. Insert the pole. If the holes don't line up perfectly, you can use a small rasp to alter the holes a bit until the pole looks as if it is aligned perfectly vertically.

How you attach the pole to your base depends on the kind of base you use. On a jumper, you need to install a 2-inch collar with an Allen wrench and a setscrew or a washer and pin, to hold the body up on the pole.

STANDS

You have to buy or make some sort of stand or platform for your animal. A variety of basic and decorative stands can be purchased from carousel supply houses, some of which are listed in Chapter 17. Some people prefer to make their own stands out of wood. If you put your animal on a platform and think you will be moving it occasionally, do yourself a favor and put casters on the platform.

PUTTYING THE JOINTS

Once your animal is glued together, you have to apply a good wood putty to all the glue joints to achieve a smooth finish. We've found it works best to apply a 1- or 1½-inch strip of putty over each glue joint, rather than simply fill gaps in the joint. This smooths out any area where the glue is stick-

ing out or has sunken in slightly. When the putty is dry, sand it down to achieve a smooth surface.

If you are planning to apply an oil or stain to your animal rather than painting it, you do not want to use putty because it will show. See Chapter 14 for directions on applying oils and stains.

Illus. 12-1.

PART THREE

Sanding and Painting Your Animal

Bravo! If you've made it this far, you should feel proud. You've built and carved your very own wooden carousel animal, using the same methods that master carvers used at the turn of the century. Your first inclination upon finishing the carving is probably to stare at your animal, show it off to your family and friends, and just bask in the glow of a great accomplishment. Go ahead, bask, you deserve it. Just try not to let this go on too long, though. If you don't put some kind of finish on your animal, some of your hard work could be ruined when the wood warps or when cracks develop at the joints, due to humidity and other environmental elements.

The following chapters explain how to seal the wood of your animal and apply an oil, stain, or paint finish. Spend some time finishing your animal. After all the work you've put into carving it, you don't want to detract from its appearance by giving the finishing stage short shrift. If you haven't done much decorative painting, practice the techniques on scrap wood that has a primer coat of paint until you feel confident.

13

Sanding

Most people hate to sand their animals, with good reason. Sanding is time-consuming, dusty, and very boring, especially on a carving as large as a full-size carousel animal. But sanding is critical to the finish of your carving. No matter how well you paint, if the surface hasn't been sanded properly, your finish is going to look amateurish.

At Horsin' Around, we've tried a variety of sanding techniques over the years and learned a few things. The most important thing we've learned is to "sand as you go," which means that as you finish carving a section of your animal (such as the mane or a leg) to your satisfaction, you sand that section before carving another section. This will break up the sanding chore and keep you from getting so bored. We don't mean carve a little area, and then sand it, and then carve a little more. If you sand before you have finished carving a section, sandpaper particles stuck in the wood fibers will quickly dull your chisels.

Another thing we've learned is to power-sand as much as possible. Most beginners spend too much time hand-sanding and quickly lose interest. In the section below, we'll explain the sanding methods that have proven fastest for us.

POWER-SANDING

The first step where sanding is useful is during the very early stages of your project when you are roughing out your animal. After roughing out the general shape of a piece, smooth the really rough parts by using a large chisel and mallet to carve away sharp edges, or a right-angle grinder with the chain-saw blade attached to "knock them down." Once this step is completed, use a power hand drill with an 80-grit sanding disk attached to smooth out areas that are still rough, to ease the carving burden and make it easier to transfer design markings to the wood. A belt sander can also be used to help level the surfaces of the joints between the head and neck, neck and body, and body and legs.

Once you have carved a section, use a Dremel tool (described in Chapter 2) to power-sand the piece. You can buy small sandpaper drums that fit your Dremel tool, or you can trace the base of a coffee cup onto cloth-backed sandpaper, and then attach the sandpaper circle to the Dremel tool to sand the body parts more easily. Be careful not to sand off all your carving detail; all you want to do is achieve a smooth surface. Also, be sure you sand evenly. You don't want to create a dip or groove by sanding too long and hard in one spot.

SANDPAPER

You can get sandpaper at any hardware or large discount store. It's worthwhile to avoid buying the cheap sandpaper, however, because it loads up quickly with sawdust, which means you will go through a lot of it without making much progress. You can identify the lower-quality sandpapers by their highly noticeable sand granules, and the fact that the grit comes off as you work.

We prefer to start out using 80-grit sandpaper, and finish up with 120 grit. We also prefer to use sandpaper with a cloth back, because it lasts longer. For hand-sanding, it can be advantageous to use some of the sanding jigs that are available in hardware stores. These jigs do things such as help you shape the sandpaper to get into tough spots, and sand evenly, so you don't inadvertently create sanding depressions in the wood.

DUST REMOVAL

One of the problems with sanding is that it produces large amounts of dust, and breathing significant amounts of wood dust can be toxic over time. Many people who do large amounts of wood-carving and other kinds of woodworking invest in dust-removal systems, which are available from any of the woodworking catalogs.

If you're on a limited budget, you can devise a simple dust-removal system of your own using a cardboard box, a box window fan, and a standard air-conditioner filter, as shown in Illus. 13-1. First, find a box that is slightly larger than your window fan, and cut off the top and bottom of the box so that it can serve as a duct. Insert the back of the fan into the box an inch or so. Then use duct tape to seal the two together on all four sides. Next, tape the filter to the other end of the box, again sealing all four sides. Make sure the fan is pulling the air through the box—away from you—as you sand in front of it.

Even if you are using a dust-removal system, it's always wise to wear a dust mask when sanding to help keep dust out of your lungs.

Illus. 13-1. **A simple dust-removal system.**

14

Sealing the Wood with Primer, Oil, or Stain

We cannot emphasize strongly enough how important it is to seal the bare wood of your animal with some type of sealer (primer if you plan to paint it, or oil or stain if you don't) as soon after carving as possible. At Horsin' Around, we've had students' animals crack when they waited too long to seal them, especially in periods of high humidity.

Before sealing your animal, you need to take these precautions:

1. Choose a work area that is well ventilated. Paints, stains, and varnishes give off fumes that can be harmful in enclosed areas. If the fumes are strong, consider using a ventilator mask (available in hardware stores) just to be safe.

2. Make sure the work area is extremely clean. You don't want dust marring your finish.

3. Cover glass eyes and jewels with masking tape before applying any finishes, to avoid ruining them.

4. Carefully clean all the sawdust and dirt from your carving before sealing and applying a finish. When it's clean, wipe all the dirt off one final time with a "tack rag"—a sticky rag that painters use to remove dust and lint from surfaces before painting.

USING PRIMER

Primer is a base paint that prepares or "primes" your wood surface for the final paint. When it's time to prime your animal, you can use a water-based primer or a lacquer primer. Both will work, but at Horsin' Around we prefer the lacquer primers because they seem to sand better when dry. We use a white lacquer primer that most people know as a stain-kill product, because it covers up stains (such as water stains) that most paints will not cover. It works well and is mildew-resistant, which helps protect your wood.

Using a primer on basswood will cause all the fibers that were loosened when you sanded your animal to rise, giving the wood a "fuzzy" feel. To diminish that fuzziness, do a thorough sanding after applying the first coat of primer.

That first sanding usually reveals little pits and obvious carving marks that catch your eye and can detract from the carving. Some people like to eliminate all the carving marks, but we feel that some of them give the animal character. To remove the unsightly marks, however, apply a red auto-body glaze, available at automotive stores, to them to even out the surface. Next, lay down another coat of white primer. When the second coat of primer is dry, lightly sand the animal as needed, and then spray on a third coat of primer to use as the base for the final paint. Spraying on the final coat makes it more even.

Here are some important guidelines about priming you should follow:

1. Don't put the primer on too thick, or it will fill in some of the finer details of your carving.

2. It's best to let each coat dry overnight, even when using a fast-drying primer. If you try to sand it before it's completely dry, the primer will clog up your sandpaper.

3. You might want to consider buying your primer in quart cans rather than larger sizes. Lacquer primers dry quickly, so once you open the can it will not last long.

4. Before you start, devise a logical order for painting the body parts, write it down, and then use that order each time you apply a coat. When painting white on white, it's very easy to get confused and miss an area. Following a set order will ensure that all the parts of your animal get an equal amount of paint.

USING OIL FINISHES

After spending so much time and effort carving their animals, some people decide they can't bear to cover their work with several layers of paint. One method of finishing that lets the wood show through is oil-finishing. A good-quality tung oil is the oil of choice; it does a great job of sealing the wood, and gives it a warm look.

To apply an oil finish, follow the directions for the brand you choose. Basswood normally requires that you rub on at least two coats. It's a good idea to use a brush to get the oil into small spots and crevices, so the whole animal is sealed. Once you have sufficiently oiled the animal, no other finish is required.

One thing to remember about oil-finishing is that while it lets the wood show through, it also reveals your mistakes. Every little carving defect will be evident, as well as any putty you used. Because of this, don't use putty if you're going to apply an oil finish.

USING A WOOD STAIN

If you want the wood to show through, but don't particularly like its color, you can seal and finish your animal with a wood stain. Before staining, you need to oil your animal with tung oil. Oiling the wood first helps ensure that you get an even stain, avoiding a blotchy look. For best results,

experiment with the stain on a piece of oiled scrap wood to get the tone you want.

Like oil finishes, wood stains let your mistakes show through the wood. Again, don't use putty if you're going to apply a wood-stain finish.

COLORED WOOD STAINS

Colored wood stains are a cross between stains and paints. The colored stain lets the wood show through, but also gives the wood a painted look. As with wood-stain finishing, you have to oil your animal before staining.

Most people using this finishing method use an oil finish or a wood-stain finish on the horseflesh, and then use colored wood stains on the trappings, saddle, figures, etc. Once again, it's wise to experiment with the colored stains on oiled pieces of scrap wood to see what a color looks like on your wood, and to determine how much stain you need to achieve the result you want.

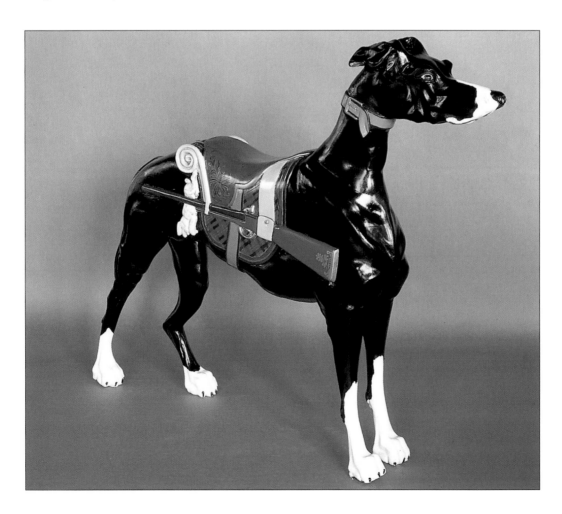

15

Final Painting

The carousel painters at the turn of the century put a lot of time and effort into blending and harmonizing the colors of the body, saddle, and trappings. They often spent hours applying gold and silver leafing to enhance the beautiful animals. After all the work you've put into carving your animal, we believe the painting of your creation deserves just as much thought and effort as the painting of the original carousel carvings.

An entire book or books could be written on painting carousel animals, so we obviously can't tell you everything there is to know about painting in this chapter. However, we can help you decide on an approach to painting your animal, and teach you a few techniques the original painters and today's professional restorers use. If you're totally inexperienced in applying decorative paint to wood, you might want to take a painting class, or get some advice from a painter in your community.

Before you even think about picking up a brush to start your final painting, you should have a clear idea of the color scheme of your animal. Basically, there are two approaches you can take: painting it with bright colors that make the animal look new, or painting it with subdued colors to make it look like an antique. If you're not sure what you like, look at photographs of restored antique animals, or visit a carousel in your area.

Once you know which approach you prefer, the best way to develop your color scheme is to make numerous copies of the pattern or tracing you used to make your blueprint, and then get some good felt-tip markers or rich-toned colored pencils and start coloring. Experiment with a variety of colors and stripes, and with gold and silver areas. Use photographs of both carousel animals and real animals to get ideas for colors. Here are a few guidelines that can help you make your color choices:

1. Stick to variations of the primary colors, rather than getting garish or going with trendy shades.

2. Avoid using too many different colors. Pick just a few colors, and use them judiciously throughout the color scheme.

3. Keep the color scheme appropriate to the animal. For example, don't use bright, flashy colors on a classic military horse.

4. If you carved your animal for display in your home, be sure to consider the lighting conditions in the area in which you plan to display it when choosing your colors, since light will affect how the colors are perceived.

CHOOSING PAINT AND BRUSHES

Carousel animals today are painted with both oils and acrylics, so you can use whichever you prefer. At Horsin' Around, we stopped using oils about six years ago because they dry slowly. You can add drying agents to oils to make them dry faster, and if you're inclined to use oils, we recommend you do precisely that, so you don't have to wait several days between applying colors. Our students prefer to use acrylics because they are faster-drying and (being water-based) easier to clean up.

Since acrylics dry so quickly, we add a drop of liquid dishwashing detergent to the paint before applying it. This slows the drying time without diluting the paint, as commercial slowing gels sometimes will. We also thin it a little with water sometimes, which also slows the drying. Since we rely on acrylics in our studio, we will primarily talk about using acrylics in the painting instructions below.

For painting small areas, we use acrylic paint straight from the container if it's the color we want, or spread some on a plastic plate if we want to mix colors. For painting large areas, we mix up a large batch (so we don't run out and have to match the color later) and put it into a clean coffee can with a plastic lid. Then we pour some into a clean glass baby-food jar so that only a small amount of the batch is exposed to the air as we paint.

Everyone has his own preference about brushes, but at Horsin' Around we prefer to use the following types of small brushes:

1. Round, heavily bristled, flat-bottomed stencil brushes that dab or "pounce" on the paint.

2. Soft, large, full-bristled mop brushes with a fanned-out shape.

3. Thin-bristled liner brushes that form a fine point.

4. Squared-off flat bristle brushes that form a fine, chisel edge.

Whatever brushes you choose to use, the most important thing to remember is that they should always be clean, not only when they are not being used but also when you are painting with them. In fact, you will probably have to stop and clean your brushes often while you are painting, to keep partially dried paint from building up on the brush and marring your stroke.

It's also important that you feel comfortable and confident using your brushes. Painting is not for the hesitant. We recommend that you prime a number of scraps of wood left over from carving your animal and practice painting on them, both to become proficient with the brushes and to test out colors and techniques before you try them on your animal.

USEFUL PAINTING TECHNIQUES

One obvious mark of amateur painting on a carousel animal is the use of one solid color to paint areas such as the flesh. The flesh or fur on a real animal is never one solid color, but is a mixture of both a variety of colors and a variety of tones. Mixing and layering colors and tones will give your animal's paint depth and richness. Below are several painting techniques that can help you achieve a nicer look.

Wet-on-Dry Painting

Applying wet paint over dry paint is a technique that is useful when adding shading or accent colors, such as around the eyes and muzzle. To use this technique, first make sure the base color is completely dry. Then use a small brush to apply some of the color to the area you are going to shade or accent.

Next, starting in the center of the wet area and working outward, vigorously move a stiff-bristled stencil brush up and down. This movement will spread out the bristles of the brush, "feathering" the paint and making the edges of the accent area blend seamlessly into the base color.

Wet-on-Wet Painting

Applying wet paint over wet paint is a technique that is used more often with oils than acrylics, because acrylics dry too quickly (unless you slow down the drying). You can use this technique in a variety of ways. For example, you can use it to blend two colors (such as painting black over white to achieve a gray shading); to blend the transition area between two colors (such as between different color patches); and to add shading (such as adding dark brown to tan to achieve a shadow effect). This technique involves using a round, mop brush to feather one paint over another.

Paint Wash

One way to get tone-on-tone effects is to use a paint wash, which is a color thinned until it goes on translucent. To make a wash, thin acrylics with water and oils with turpentine. To apply a wash, use a flat, dry brush to lightly brush it over another color that is completely dry.

Dry-Brushing

Dry-brushing is best done with a flat brush. First, put a dab of paint (no water added) on your palette and work the brush back and forth through the paint. Then pat the brush on a paper towel to remove almost all the paint. Finally, when the excess paint has been removed, apply the leftover paint to the surface with a light touch.

Stippling

Stippling gives a textured look. To stipple, vigorously move a dry brush up and down on the wood's surface.

Shading and Highlighting

Shading is a technique that adds a darker tone to recessed areas, which normally would not get as much light. Highlighting is a technique that adds a lighter tone to an area (usually a "high" area) to "bring it forward" so that it looks as if the area is receiving the most light. To shade, use a dry brush to brush on a darker color or add a dark tone over a lighter color. To highlight, use a dry brush to brush on a lighter color or add a lighter tone to a darker color. (You can even do this several times, lightening the shade each time.)

STARTING POINTS

It's useful to plan the painting order before you begin. At Horsin' Around, we spray on our last coat of primer to serve as the smooth base for the final coat. We then paint in this order: 1) body flesh, 2) face and head, 3) mane and tail, 4) gold leafing (if any), 5) saddle and trappings, and 6) hoofs. After that, we apply the clear finish coats, add the striping, and paint the horseshoes.

Painting the Flesh/Body

As mentioned above, no flesh color on an animal consists of one solid color. Below are some common horseflesh colors and directions on how to achieve them.

White, Gray, and Palomino There are actually two different shades of white horse: yellow- and gray-toned. To achieve yellow-toned flesh, add a small amount of ocher to the white base paint. To achieve gray-toned flesh, add a small amount of black to the white base paint.

Before you apply the flesh color, stipple light-pink undertones (made by mixing a little red into your white base paint) under the chin, the tail, and where the underbelly meets the legs. Then thin the flesh color to make a wash, and lightly brush the wash over all the flesh. (You can leave white primer on the underbelly and the inside areas of the legs.)

When the wash is dry, use a 1-inch-wide stencil brush to dab on a darker flesh color (made by adding more ocher or black) to areas that need shading, such as the recesses of muscles, and a lighter flesh color to areas that need highlighting. Remember that you are trying to achieve flesh with very subtle variations, not a completely uniform look.

Palomino flesh is just a yellow-toned white with more ocher added, and gray flesh is gray-toned white with more black added. When painting palomino or gray flesh, stipple the same pink undertones as described above for white flesh before you add the flesh color. Then use a stencil brush to dab on the flesh color all over the body, using a darker tone of the same color for shading and a lighter tone for highlighting.

Black Like white flesh, black flesh also has two different shades: blue-black and brown-black.

Both are achieved most easily with acrylic paint. For blue-black flesh, first apply a coat of pure cobalt blue to areas that will be black, including the underbelly and inside areas of the legs. Using a stencil brush, add a darker tone (made by adding a little black) to areas that need shading, and a lighter tone (made by adding a little white) to areas that need highlighting. When the blue has completely dried, thin some black paint to make a wash and brush it over the blue.

For brown-black flesh, first apply a coat of burnt sienna to the areas that will be black, adding darker and lighter tones as needed. When the burnt sienna has completely dried, brush a thinned black wash over it, using the methods described above.

Brown There are so many shades and tones of brown that you will have to experiment to find the combination that makes the brown you desire. Some colors you can mix to make different shades of brown include ocher, naples yellow, and burnt sienna. To make the brown flesh look realistic, use yellow ocher as a base paint, and then brush the brown wash over it.

Dapple Gray Dapple gray is a popular flesh color, but it is a very time-consuming effect to achieve. To make dapple gray flesh, first paint the flesh a shade of gray. Then dip half of a wide, dry brush in creamy-white paint and the other half in a different shade. Next, stipple in a tight circle, putting the lighter-colored paint on the inside. This procedure will blend the light and dark colors, giving a dappled effect. When painting dapple-gray flesh, put the dapples sparingly on the sides, rump, and flank. Leave the underbelly and inside area of the legs white primer.

One last note on horseflesh paint: The original carousel painters painted the flesh color onto the edge of any trapping or decorations that bordered the flesh area. This technique helped disguise edges that were not carved perfectly, and helped sharpen the finished look.

Painting the Face and Head

If you look at the face photographs in the Carving Galleries and in books about antique carousel horses, you'll notice that most carousel horses have shading around their eyes. The color is usually a darker shade of the flesh-tone paint, often the same darker shade used to shade the recesses of muscles.

To shade the eyes, use a small liner brush to carefully apply the paint to the area immediately surrounding the eye. Then feather the paint outward so it gets lighter and lighter as it spreads out. When the eye area is completely dry, remove the masking tape protecting the glass eye. With a small liner brush, carefully paint the tear duct in the inner corner of the eye a light pink.

To give your paint more depth, you can also use the darker shade of flesh-tone paint (or a contrasting color) to shade the recessed areas around the muzzle.

Next, paint the inside of the mouth, nostrils, and ears. To do this, thin some light-pink paint, and use a stencil brush to dab it on the inside of each cavity. Then dry the brush a little, and stipple a little pink around the outer edges of the lips and the muzzle. The pink should be barely visible. When the mouth area has completely dried, use a small brush to paint the teeth white.

Painting the Mane and Tail

If you look at manes and tails on antique animals, you'll see that some carousel horse manes are smooth, and some are textured to look more like real hair. To paint a smooth mane or tail, brush the mane color over the whole mane. Then add a darker shade of the same color in some of the recessed areas so the hair is not all one color. To paint a textured mane or tail, brush on a slightly thinned-down shade of your mane color, then use a dry, stiff brush to firmly wipe away the excess paint. This leaves slight texture lines, and even lets a little of the base color show through.

To paint the mane, start at its tip and work upward, following the carving line. To paint the tail, start at the body and work downward, also following the carving line. If you are using acrylic paint, you will need to work quickly to firmly wipe away the excess paint before it dries. You can then add a darker shade of the same color in the recessed areas, as in the smooth mane.

Gold/Silver Leafing

At Horsin' Around, we usually apply gold and silver leafing after we paint the body, but before we paint the saddle and trappings. Then we put a complementary color wash over the leafing. If you plan to do some metal leafing, make sure the surface you intend to leaf is sanded perfectly smooth. Then add a couple of coats of shellac to the area, to give the leafing a better surface to adhere to.

You'll need to follow the specific directions for whatever metal leafing product you buy, but the basics are simple (although you need to proceed carefully). First, brush on a glue called sizing, and then wait until it dries to a "tacky" state. A good indicator that a glue is tacky is when you touch it with your knuckle and your knuckle sticks slightly, and then lets go with a "popping" sound. If any sizing comes off on your skin when you touch it, it's still too wet.

Once the sizing is tacky, lay the metal leafing on the wood (working from bottom to top), overlapping the sheets slightly, until the surface is covered. As soon as you complete the leafing, "burnish" it by brushing over it gently with a soft brush until it develops the proper shine.

The original carousel painters often used a shortcut gold-leafing method that was cheaper and faster than true gold leafing. It involves brushing orange shellac over a silvered surface. First, cover the surface with silver leaf or silver paint, and let it dry thoroughly. Next, varnish the area and let it dry for 24 hours. Finally, mix two-thirds orange shellac to one-third shellac thinner, and brush the shellac mixture over the area. If you are covering a large flat area with this method, consider using a spray shellac so your brush strokes don't show. Be sure to mask everything around the area you are working on, however, before you spray.

Painting the Saddle and Trappings

Painting the trappings is basically a matter of mixing the colors to match your planned color scheme, and carefully brushing the paint on. Saddles and other "leather" sections are painted black, brown, or white. To make the saddle look like real brown leather, we usually begin by painting the leather area orange. Then we use a stencil brush to dab on the brown base-color paint, and stipple a darker shade of the same color around the edges. Use this same technique on other leather parts, such as the cinch and harness.

Painting the Hoofs

If you look at a real horse, you will see that its hoofs are striated rather than smooth. To achieve this look with paint, brush on the slightly thinned-down hoof color, then use a stiff, dry brush to firmly remove the excess paint and leave a slight texture. Brush from the top of the hoof down. A good color for the hoofs is the same color you used to shade the recessed areas on the face and body, or a contrasting color that was used on the muzzle.

CLEAR FINISH

After the basic painting is completed, you need to apply several coats of a clear protective finish. Most people use spar varnish, which dries very hard. However, varnish yellows over time. We've had good luck with a clear finish designed for wood floors. Whatever you use, try it out first on a painted piece of scrap wood to make sure it works with your paint and you like the effect.

STRIPING

Painting the grooves or veins you carved as saddle or trapping decoration is called striping. Striping needs to stand out, but shouldn't clash with the colors on the large painted areas. Instead, it should be used to complement all the other colors.

Striping is painted with a liner brush. Since you paint the striping over the clear finish, it's a good idea to remove some paint from the container and mix in a few drops of the finish with the color to make sure that the paint and finish bind well before you paint your animal.

When striping, you might want to try a technique that the original carousel painters used. If your grooves and veining are not perfectly carved (as most aren't), place the liner brush tip inside the carved groove. Then apply enough pressure to cause the paint to flow in an even-width line that goes up over both edges of the groove. Doing this creates a visual illusion, causing the eye to believe the carved groove is of a consistent width and depth, even when in reality it might have variations.

SADDLE-STITCHING

Some people like to add simulated "stitching" to their saddles to make them look more realistic. To do this, carve a small groove where the stitching will go, and then punch small holes in the groove in an evenly spaced pattern. Stretch the string over the groove, and then put the string and a little glue into each hole. After you have finished, cover the string with Krazy glue to protect it.

HORSESHOES

If you carved your horseshoes, you have to paint them silver. We use an acrylic silver paint, but any good silver paint will work.

PAINTING INSTRUCTIONS FOR MENAGERIE ANIMAL CARVERS

You can use the same painting techniques and approaches described for painting horses to paint your menagerie animal. The biggest difference will be that—depending on your animal—you will probably want your paint scheme to look very realistic, especially if your animal has no trappings. Rely on photographs of your animal, both in carousel form and in real life, for guidance. Pay particular attention to the appropriateness of your color choices. Wrong choices can make menagerie animals look cartoonish.

PART FOUR

Organ Figures
and Carving
Resources

We offer this part of the book as a lagniappe—a small gift in appreciation of your interest in our book and in carousel art. In Chapter 16, we provide some patterns for two antique band-organ figures, the wonder- ful little figures that adorn carousel organs. After carving a full-size carousel animal, carving an organ figure should be no prob- lem for you. In Chapter 17, we provide a limited list of carving resources, to help you with your project.

16

Carving an Organ Figure

Carvers interested in carousels are not only carving carousel animals, they are also carving reproductions of the wonderful old band-organ figures. There were a wide variety of figures adorning the original carousel band organs.

Illus. 16-1 and 16-2 are patterns for two Gavioli band-organ figures, one a man and one a woman. Front and side views are provided, so you can draw both views on your block of wood. The original figures were about 18 to 22 inches tall. You carve them using the same techniques you used to carve your carousel animal.

Each figure has a movable arm. The original figures had arms that moved by mechanical wire. Today's organs move the figures by using air pressure, either by blowing the air or by creating a vacuum. The arm is designed to hang down from gravity, and then go up on a rhythm note. To make the arm of the figure move, follow the instructions below.

MAKING THE ARM MOVE

First, carve the arm in the relaxed position (Illus. 16-3 and 16-4). Then use a fine-toothed saw to cut out a wedge at the elbow joint, as shown in Illus. 16-5. Next, drill a hole through the stationary upper part of the arm above the elbow joint, through to where you cut out the wedge. Insert a metal tube in the hole, and seal the hole around it with a good sealant so air can't move between the outer diameter of the metal tube and the hole.

Now, put a metal hinge at the point of the wedge you cut out. Take some thin leather, and fasten it horizontally around the elbow joint. The leather needs to be loose enough so that the arm can hang down because of gravity, but it needs to be attached to the wood with a sealant so you get a vacuum seal. Then attach a plastic tube to the metal tube. The plastic tube can be attached to a vacuum source, which will raise the arm by creating a vacuum (Illus. 16-6).

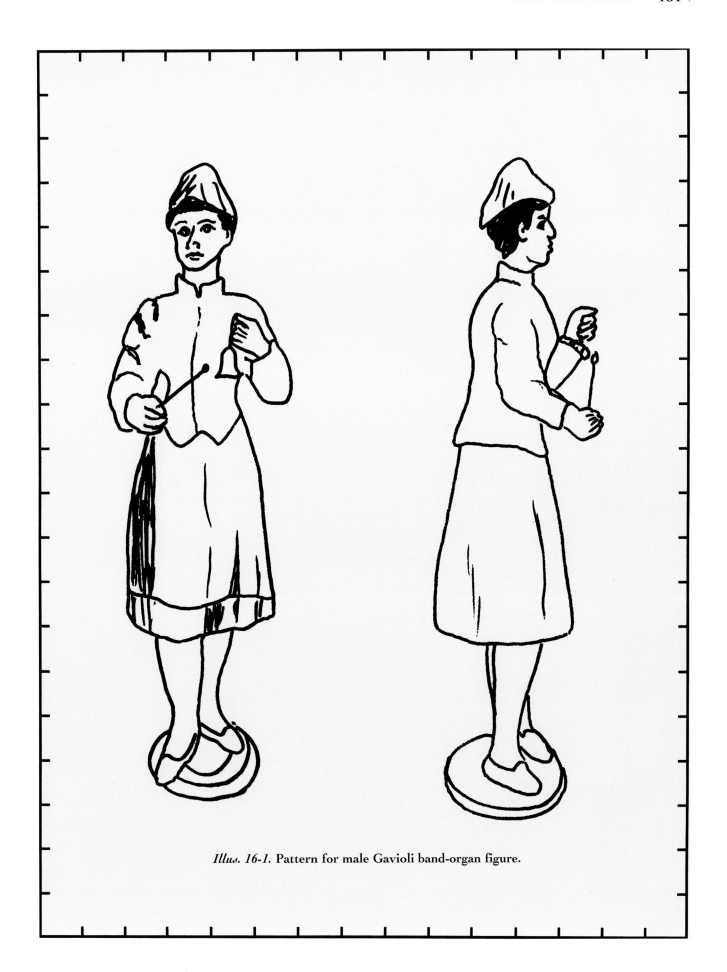

Illus. 16-1. Pattern for male Gavioli band-organ figure.

Illus. 16-2. **Pattern for female Gavioli band-organ figure.**

Illus. 16-3. A carved blank for a band-organ figure is cut out and laminated using the same techniques that are used on a carousel animal.

Illus. 16-4. After the pattern markings have been transferred to the organ figure, it can be roughed out with an angle grinder to remove excess wood.

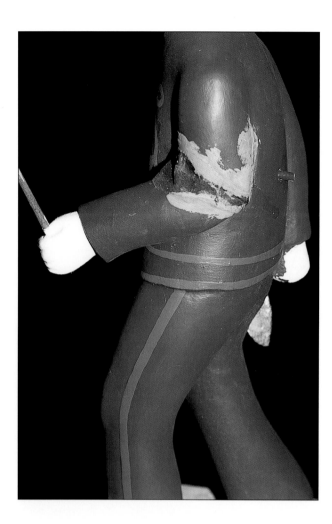

Illus. 16-5.

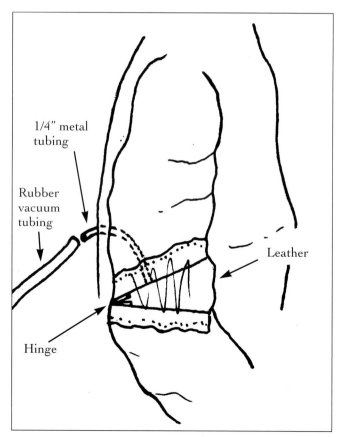

Illus. 16-6. **Most old band-organ figures worked by a mechanical wire. Many organs today work by air pressure either blowing or operated by a vacuum source. The figure's arm would normally hang down because of gravity and would be vacuumed up on a rhythm note.**

1/4" metal tubing

Rubber vacuum tubing

Leather

Hinge

Illus. 16-7. Painting a band-organ figure.

17

Carving Resources

Following is a list of carving resources that you might find useful as you carve and paint your carousel animal. This list is by no means exhaustive. For the most up-to-date sources, consult a carousel trade publication.

CAROUSEL PUBLICATIONS

Carousel News & Trader
87 Park Avenue West, Suite 206
Mansfield, OH 44902
419-529-4999

PATTERNS AND BLUEPRINTS

Horsin' Around
3804 St. Elmo Ave.
Chattanooga, TN 37409
423-825-5616

K.B. Leather Art
Kathleen Bond
2341 Irwin Rd.
Holland, OH 43528-9732
419-829-2933

Zon International Publishing Co.
P.O. Box 6459
Santa Fe, NM 87502
800-266-5767

JEWELS AND GLASS EYES

Janet Berwin
2111 Plattin Rd.
Festus, MO 63028
314-937-6998

Van Dyke Supply Co. Inc.
Dept. 30087
P.O. Box 278
Woonsocket, SD 57385
800-843-3320

HORSEHAIR TAILS

Flying Tails
June Reely
1209 Indiana Ave.
S. Pasadena, CA 91030
213-256-8657

J&M Carousel
1711 Calavaras Dr.
Santa Rosa, CA 95405
800-789-1026

Sally Craig
336 West High St.
Elizabethtown, PA 17022
717-367-4616

BRASS SLEEVES AND FINIALS/STANDS

Carousel Memories
P.O. Box 33225
Los Gatos, CA 95031
408-356-2306

The Bed Post
32 S. High St.
Dept. C
E. Bangor, PA 18013
610-588-4667

Automatic Tubing Corp.
888 Lorimer St.
Brooklyn, NY 11222-3990
800-527-3091 (Outside New York)
718-383-0100 (In New York)

CARVING CRAFT SUPPLIES

Cast Iron Carousel Animal Stands
417 Valley Road
Madison, WI 53714
608-222-1100

CAROUSEL ORGANIZATIONS

American Carousel Society
3845 Telegraph Rd.
Elkton, MD 21921
410-392-4289

National Carousel Association
P.O. Box 4333
Evansville, IN 47724-0333

National Carnival Association
P.O. Box 4165
Salisbury, NC 28145-4165

CAROUSEL MUSEUMS

Herschell Carrousel Factory Museum
180 Thompson St.
North Tonawanda, NY 14120
716-693-1885

American Carousel Museum
Traveling Carousel Exhibits
655 Beach St., Suite 400
San Francisco, CA 94109
415-928-0550

Carousel World Museum
Routes 202 and 263
Lahaska, PA 18931
215-794-8960

Dickinson County Heritage Center
412 S. Campbell
Abilene, KS 67410-2905
913-263-2681

International Museum of Carousel Art
500 North Second St.
Hood River, OR 97031
503-387-2979

The Merry-Go-Round Museum
West Washington & Jackson St.
P.O. Box 718
Sandusky, OH 44870
419-626-6111

New England Carousel Museum
95 Riverside Ave.
Bristol, CT 06010
860-585-5411

CAROUSEL SITES ON THE WORLDWIDE WEB

The Carousel Organization
http://www.carousel.org
http://www.carousel.net

The Carousel News & Trader
http://www.carousel.net/trader

METRIC EQUIVALENCY CHART
mm—millimetres   cm—centimetres
INCHES TO MILLIMETRES AND CENTIMETRES

inches	mm	cm	inches	cm	inches	cm
⅛	3	0.3	9	22.9	30	76.2
¼	6	0.6	10	25.4	31	78.7
⅜	10	1.0	11	27.9	32	81.3
½	13	1.3	12	30.5	33	83.8
⅝	16	1.6	13	33.0	34	86.4
¾	19	1.9	14	35.6	35	88.9
⅞	22	2.2	15	38.1	36	91.4
1	25	2.5	16	40.6	37	94.0
1¼	32	3.2	17	43.2	38	96.5
1½	38	3.8	18	45.7	39	99.1
1¾	44	4.4	19	48.3	40	101.6
2	51	5.1	20	50.8	41	104.1
2½	64	6.4	21	53.3	42	106.7
3	76	7.6	22	55.9	43	109.2
3½	89	8.9	23	58.4	44	111.8
4	102	10.2	24	61.0	45	114.3
4½	114	11.4	25	63.5	46	116.8
5	127	12.7	26	66.0	47	119.4
6	152	15.2	27	68.6	48	121.9
7	178	17.8	28	71.1	49	124.5
8	203	20.3	29	73.7	50	127.0

INDEX